# NATIONALISM AND
# AMERICAN CATHOLICISM

# NATIONALISM AND AMERICAN CATHOLICISM

*by DOROTHY DOHEN*

*with an Introduction by*
*JOSEPH P. FITZPATRICK, S.J.*

SHEED AND WARD : NEW YORK

*In memory of W. J. D.*

# Contents

# Introduction

In recent statements Father John Courtney Murray has centered his attention on two themes: 1) the singular accomplishment of the American experience; it has achieved a separation of State from Church which strongly secures the right of the Church to be free; and 2) the singular task which still confronts that experience, namely, the need to clarify the relation of the sacred to the secular in a nation in which they are separate. This latter is a complicated and delicate task. Father Murray suggests that Catholic scholars who have shared the American experience will have a unique advantage in seeking to define the relation of the sacred to the secular as modern political structures emerge. The publication of Dorothy Dohen's book is convincing evidence that Catholic scholars are competently and conscientiously busy at their task. Using as a case study the development of a fusion of religion and nationalism in the experience of Catholics in the United States, Professor Dohen has given us an analysis of the relation of sacred to secular which is illuminating as well as frightening. It focuses on the subtle dangers to which sincere and zealous guardians of the sacred are exposed unless they are continuously vigilant about the strange direction which social and political actualities can give to what initially may be the purest religious plans and intentions.

The relationship of the Church to the world is the enduring problem of Christianity. Central to this problem is the problem of nationality. It is no mystery that the most precise revelation given by God to the Church after the ascension of Our Lord was directed to the problem of nationality. Cornelius, an officer of the Roman army of occupation in Palestine, was the first uncircumcised Gentile to ask for baptism, and his request raised the crucial question: Were members of other nations to be required to accept the Hebrew way of life (the Mosaic Law) in order to be Christians? Or were they to continue to live according to their own way of life after baptism? "God has been showing me," Peter explained on the occasion, "that He makes no distinction between man and man; He welcomes anybody, whatever his race [or, as we would say, his culture or nationality] who fears him and does what piety demands (Acts 10:34–5)." Probably the first case of culture-shock among Christians is reported in relation to the same episode: "The faithful who had come over with Peter, holding to the tradition of circumcision as they did, were astonished to find that the free gift of the Holy Spirit could be lavished on the Gentiles whom they heard speaking with tongues and proclaiming the greatness of God (*ibid.,* 45–6)." In other words, the Spirit could express himself just as well among people who lived according to a Roman way of life or a Greek or Egyptian way of life as He could among those who lived according to the Hebrew way of life. The Church was never to be identified with any culture or any nation. This was the freedom of the children of God under the new law.

The episode indicated that the problem of culture and nationality was to be a troublesome issue for the Church. It became the major issue at the First Council of Jerusalem (Acts 15). But despite the clear declarations of the Apostles about the freedom of the Gentiles, the problem remained to unsettle and almost tear apart the early Church. It has continued to trouble the Church ever since. It remained, twenty centuries later, a major issue at the Second Vatican Council. Christians have an almost irresistible tendency to identify their faith with their own culture and their own nation. In doing so, they threaten to restrict its catholicity, confine its expression within the narrow limits of a single culture or nation, and ultimately destroy the universality which enables the life and word of God to be meaningful to men of all times and all nationalities.

Therefore, one desperate need of the Church at every moment of her history has been the need to distinguish that which is essential to the Faith, and that which is its transitory cultural, historical, or national expression. This need now finds a helpful instrument in the methods and concepts of the social sciences which, in recent generations, have been able to give us a deepening insight into the nature of culture, the nature of the nation State, and the relationship between the State and a variety of institutions which dynamically constitute its life. Professor Dohen's work represents a continuing effort to use the methods of the social sciences to analyze the relationship between the Church and its cultural and national expression in the United States. It is precisely this careful study of the emerging relation of the sacred to the secular in the American experience which Father Murray called for, and which will be essential if the Church is to arrive at a vital relationship to the American nation which will represent a creative religious and civil achievement rather than a troublesome entanglement.

For example, it had appeared that the development of a religiously pluralistic society in the United States would eliminate the difficulties of the identification of religion with nation. Actually, if the author's thesis is correct, it has had the opposite effect. The American experience, as she explains it, has been characterized by a tendency to identify sacred symbols with secular ones, national goals with religious goals in such a way that the nation tends to become accepted as the ultimate arbiter in human affairs. In this situation, religion may be reduced to a point where it simply reinforces national goals and values; it becomes nothing but a social function and loses its prophetic role of calling God to witness the works of men. This secularization of religion, to which so many contemporary writers call our attention, was the very thing which separation of Church and State was expected to prevent. Scholars who have analyzed this dilemma have generally suggested that it resulted from the experience of immigration. Professor Dohen, however, locates its origin basically in the very effort to achieve a religiously pluralistic society. The loss of common religious symbols to express the common values and goals of the nation gives rise to a tendency to project a sacred character into the national values and goals themselves. This results in the fusion of religion and nationalism which she examines in her book.

This is a significant sociological insight. It implies that, in the development of a nation like the United States, the problem for the sacred has not arisen because the State was too separated from the Church; it arose because the State was not separated enough. The guardians of the sacred did not find it possible to allow the State to be genuinely secular. If this insight is correct, it has profound implications for political officials and for religious leaders.

The major part of this book is a case study of the Catholic experience in the United States. It would be a serious mistake to infer from this that the problem is specifically a Catholic problem or even specifically an American problem. On the contrary, relating the sacred to the secular is a universal religious problem. The value of this case study is the light that it may shed on the problem in general. Furthermore, due to the fact that the United States has had such extensive experience with religious pluralism, this kind of study by scholars in the United States can make a unique contribution to an increasing understanding of the problem anywhere in the world.

The author constructs her case study out of the examination of the public statements of six Catholic bishops, archbishops, and cardinals who were chosen as recognized representatives of Catholic opinion at successive moments in the history of the Catholic Church in the United States. It would be regrettable if this were interpreted simply as a criticism of the hierarchy. It is rather a remarkably documented analysis of the challenges, the struggles, the efforts at creative response which were characteristic of the hierarchy as its members sought to bring the Church into a dynamic relationship with the American nation. The book reflects a deep respect on Professor Dohen's part for the social, cultural, political and religious contexts in which the bishops were acting.

What emerges from the analysis is a clearer recognition of the subtle way in which sincere attempts to relate religion to social and political forces can result in dilemmas for the Church, apparently without the churchmen or their flocks being aware of it. For example, the fusion of religion and nationalism began as a Protestant phenomenon. But this Protestant response of the sacred to the secular was quickly absorbed by Catholics in their effort to become identified as American. Or again, when the Catholic bishops sought to protect the Church from the nationalism of its numerous immigrant groups of communicants, they tended to create an equally strong nationalistic attachment to the United States.

Troublesome dilemmas of this kind may affect any religious

group as it seeks to relate itself to a modern State; and other dilemmas, more serious and complicated, will surely arise. What is needed, therefore, is continued study and analysis of the complex interplay of religious, social, and political forces which affect the efforts of men to express their faith in a meaningful way in the world of which they are a part. This marks out more sharply the task of which Father Murray speaks and which Miss Dohen has attempted, namely, the task of defining the relation of the sacred to the secular in a nation in which both are separate. It also marks out her book as one more step in the slow and laborious effort toward a competent, helpful and contemporary sociology of religion.

JOSEPH P. FITZPATRICK, S.J.
*Professor of Sociology*
*Fordham University*

# 1/"Right or Wrong, My Country"

On December 23, 1965, Cardinal Spellman, arriving in South Vietnam for a five-day Christmas visit, was asked by newsmen: "What do you think about what the United States is doing in Vietnam?" He answered, "I fully support everything it does." Then, paraphrasing the words of the nineteenth-century naval hero, Stephen Decatur, the Cardinal added, "My country, may it always be right. Right or wrong, my country."[1]

These words may not have seemed startling when uttered by a hero of the military establishment, but they do seem out of character for a high-ranking prelate of the universal Church. Do they represent a mere slip of the tongue on his part, readily understandable as a response to the unexpected in an unscheduled press interview? His words were allowed to stand; no attempt was made to correct the impression given by this interview; and no subsequent press release was issued to dispel the notion of an attitude of uncritical nationalism. The implication, then, may be drawn that the Cardinal's reply does indeed reflect rather accurately his mind on the subject.

Expressions of nationalism are not idiosyncratic to Cardinal Spellman as a religious leader. A number of writers have noted the way in which adherents of traditional religion in

America have unthinkingly accepted and made ready adjustments to nationalism, and several articulate Protestant theologians have remarked that nationalism in the United States has captured the transcendental note of religion. Thus Martin E. Marty writes that among religious Americans "Democracy becomes the ultimate, religion the handmaiden,"[2] while another Protestant theologian, Kyle Haselden, speaks of "the fashionable, conventional, patriotic folk-faith which today displaces pristine Christianity and Judaism as the nation's religion . . ."[3] H. Richard Niebuhr likewise expressed his concern about "the bondage of the church to nationalism," and he characterized nationalism itself as "so evidently a religion."[4]

Another concerned critic of modern American nationalism is Will Herberg. Since the first publication of *Protestant-Catholic-Jew* in 1955, Herberg has been at pains to develop his thesis that the "formally unacknowledged, but very potent religion" of America is "the religion of the American Way of Life."[5] In the following passage he illustrates his contention that the nation has superseded religion in providing the ultimate means of identification for Americans.

. . . I recently lectured to the entire student body of a well-known Catholic girls' college. In the course of my remarks, I confronted them—not in such a way as to put them on their guard, of course—with Christopher Dawson's celebrated question: "Are you Americans who happen to be Catholics, or Catholics who happen to be Americans?" Almost with one voice the girls answered, "Americans who happen to be Catholics. . . ." You appreciate the significance of the question and the answer. The question really means: "Is your ultimate allegiance and your ultimate community the Universal Church, or is it the American nation?" The answer of the girls indicated that they normally thought of themselves as primarily Americans, but of course as Americans of "the Catholic kind," just as some of their friends were Americans of "the Protestant kind," and still others Americans of "the Jewish kind." . . .[6]

Thus Herberg sees the specific religions of Protestantism, Judaism and Catholicism as having become socially-accepted ways of belonging to an overarching "common religion."

In evident agreement with the theologians that nationalism in the modern world has become a religion is the historian Carlton J. H. Hayes who devoted much of his professional career to the exploration of the interplay of religion and nationalism. He concludes that "Syncretism of nationalism and religion is strikingly noticeable in the United States."[7] Daniel Bell, a sociologist, has commented on the union of nationalism and traditional religion in the Christian Front movements of the radical right.[8] Two other historians who have noted the nationalism present specifically in American Catholicism are Richard Hofstadter[9] and Henry J. Browne.[10]

Impressionistic evidence of the presence of nationalism in American Catholicism has been observed. For example, it is probably not without significance that six of the seven published works of Cardinal Spellman are on patriotic themes and seem to display an uncritical acceptance of national goals.[11] Nationalism, it is asserted, has even crept into more properly spiritual books: a sociological analysis of popular religious and inspirational literature comments on the nationalistic spirit of such Catholic writers as Bishop Fulton J. Sheen and Father James Keller.[12]

WHAT IS NATIONALISM?

It is interesting to note that many writers who discuss nationalism do so without stopping to consider what they mean by the term. Indeed, it has been remarked that historians, although uncertain of what nationalism means, have described the process by which nationalism has reshaped the modern world.[13]

Evidently *nationalism* is something more than mere *patriotism*; but what is this "something more"? The inscription "For God and Country" often inscribed on the façade of Catholic schools in the United States is an expression of loyalty to and love for country; but is it an expression of patriotism or of nationalism? How does one distinguish between the two?

Pope Pius XI attempted to make such a distinction in *Ubi Arcano*:

> For this patriotism and national loyalty, though a potent spur to many virtues and brave deeds as long as it is guided by the law of Christ, becomes nevertheless the source of widespread wrongs and evils when it oversteps the bounds of justice and right and grows into excessive nationalism [*immoderatum nationis amorem*].

He thus distinguishes nationalism from the well-ordered love of country which observes due proportion. This love, *caritas patriae*, he sees as being quite different from nationalism.

Martin Buber aptly describes the difference when he writes:

> Being a people is simply like having eyes in one's head which are capable of seeing; being a nationality is like having learned to perceive their function and to understand their purpose; nationalism is having diseased eyes and hence being constantly preoccupied with the fact of having eyes. A people is a phenomenon of life, nationality (which cannot exist without national feeling) is one of consciousness, nationalism one of superconsciousness.[14]

Here, evidently, Buber is not only implying a distinction between a national consciousness which he considers legitimate and one which he apparently evaluates as illegitimate ("nationalism is having diseased eyes"), but he is also pointing out the intensity which the adherents of nationalism can exhibit.

It is very difficult to arrive at a definition of nationalism which will recognize this powerful emotional component without, at the same time, provoking the vehement disagreement of those who may, in fact, themselves be nationalistic. For instance, consider Boyd Shafer's implied definition of nationalism: "In the contemporary world men identify themselves first by their nationality, act primarily in their national groupings, and generally worship national ideals above all others."[15] Now, while Shafer may mean this to be accurate, descriptive and emotionally neutral, the phrase *"worship* national ideals," which may be a rather exact description of the devotion of those who espouse nationalism, would probably be unacceptable to and provoke the hostility of those nationalists who are, at the same time, adherents to traditional religion: it seems to attack the norms to which they subscribe, even though it may nicely describe their actual behavior.

Less objectionable is Shafer's eventual definition: "The devotion that men give to their nations, their national interests and ideals, their nation-states is called nationalism."[16] However, it seems to fail as an ideal definition of nationalism since it does not specify the nature of this "devotion" to the nation, nor does it relate it to other areas of man's identification.

Gerth and Mills define nationalism as "the justifying ideology of the nation-state or of a nation aspiring to become a state."[17] This definition is valuable because it covers the ideology of both those nations who have achieved statehood as well as the ideology of those nations (people with common cultural origins) who aspire to such political independence. However, the definition of Gerth and Mills, like Shafer's definition, fails, since it does not specify the character of the ideology of the nation-state in relationship to other—and possibly competing—ideologies.

K. H. Silvert has arrived at a definition which seems valuable in this respect: "Nationalism is the acceptance of the state as the impersonal and ultimate arbiter of human affairs."[18] Silvert notes that, while his definition seems quite bald, its implications are broad: it describes the prime function of the nation-state, and names it as the institutionalized means of power, while it implies the necessity of the loyal participation of the citizenry in terms "over-riding primary loyalties to intermediate family, religious, or other competing areas of identification."[19] However, Silvert's definition, mentioning as it does "the acceptance of the *state*," seems to overemphasize the political community to the neglect of the cultural community. Moreover, it does not give attention to the ideological character of nationalism.

In this present study which is inevitably concerned with values and the possible conflict between national and religious values, a definition which brings out the value dimension of nationalism is preferable. For this reason, the writer has chosen to construct her own definition which borrows heavily from both the definition of nationalism given by Gerth and Mills and the one given by Silvert: *Nationalism is the ideology which permits the nation to be the impersonal and final arbiter of human affairs.* This definition brings out the point that nationalism encourages the nation to view its common value system as ultimate, at the same time that it conceives of the nation as the best single interpreter of the common creed or value system.[20] This definition of nationalism—like Silvert's —in stressing that the nation is the "final arbiter," gives it a role in human affairs which has priority over the role of religion, since in cases of value conflict it is the nation—not religion—which has the ultimate right to interpret its own creed, as well as to judge its own actions.

## "THE ONLY RELIGIOUS PEOPLE"

When religious people and religious leaders in the United States are thought to be nationalistic, is there any evidence that they really have accepted the nation as final arbiter? And, if so, how strong is the evidence? Certainly it would seem that unquestioning acceptance of the nation's actions, whether they are "right or wrong," would give evidence of nationalism. But the words—and even the behavior—of one prelate would not prove the presence of nationalism in American Catholicism. A more thorough investigation of the American Catholic experience is needed. However, such an investigation can be pursued only after we have first established the context in which American Catholicism has developed.

The paradox of nationalism in America co-existing with evident religious fervor (as manifested through religious practice) has been noted by Herberg, but actually it was remarked upon over a century before by one of the most astute visitors ever to come to our shores. Indeed, on his visit to the United States in 1830, Tocqueville remarked on the great religiosity of the American people and spoke with some annoyance over their feeling that they were, in fact, "the only religious . . . people."[21] He further commented on what he considered the strange relationship of their religion to their patriotism. Noting that Americans regard religion as the support of and the means to their democratic ends, Tocqueville wrote: "In America, religion is the road to knowledge, and the observance of the divine law leads men to civil liberty."[22]

American democracy, Tocqueville recognized, turned to

religion as the source of its legitimation; religion, he observed, gave Americans the source of their integration as a nation.[23] But the question intrudes itself here: Why religion? Why did Americans, evidently from the earliest days of the foundation of the United States, turn to religion to symbolize and promote their social integration even while, at the same time, they were deliberately de-institutionalizing religion politically and proclaiming freedom of religious choice? The answer to this particular question seems to depend on a historical explanation to be offered in the following chapter.

From the founding of our nation to the present, to be an American has meant to be religious; at the same time, some rather odd consequences have followed the American conviction that the specific contents of one's religious beliefs is nobody's business. Some of these are exhibited today: for instance, the wedding of Christianity and nationalism in such movements as the Christian Front and such organizations as the Minute Men. A supposed attack on religion is interpreted to be an attack on the nation. There seems to be a frenetic clinging to the symbols of religion and religious formulations as a mark of national identity and security, even when these symbols and formulations have become so garbled as to be theologically meaningless. Thus the sign "Keep God in America," displayed on automobile bumpers during the Goldwater-Johnson campaign, betrayed not only theological confusion and a certain lack of lived religious experience (because people who live in the immediacy of God would be hard put to conceive such a slogan), but also a rather desperate effort to hold onto religious symbols because of the feeling that, without them, the nation will perish.

In contrast to the nationalism which hates religion or overthrows religion of the traditional variety, this type of nationalism seems to exalt it; but it first empties it of specific religious content.[24]

What accounts for the peculiar admixture of religion and nationalism in America? Or, to ask it another way, what is the genesis of the particular American form of nationalism?

This is a question to which we must address ourselves before we can examine—let alone understand—how nationalism developed in American Catholicism.

## NOTES

[1] As reported in a dispatch from Saigon in the *New York Times*, Dec. 24, 1965. Rev. Patrick O'Connor, in an NC dispatch from Saigon, reports the same interview with little variation.

The Cardinal was asked why he had come. "This year," he answered, "I want to show my loyalty to what my country is doing for peace. As Stephen Decatur said," he added, " 'My country, right or wrong.' "

[2] Martin E. Marty, *The New Shape of American Religion* (New York: Harper, 1959), p. 78.

[3] Kyle Haselden, "Introduction," in Kyle Haselden and Martin E. Marty, eds., *What's Ahead for the Churches*? A Report from *The Christian Century* (New York: Sheed and Ward, 1964), p. 4.

[4] H. Richard Niebuhr, "Independence of the Church," in H. Shelton Smith, Robert T. Handy, Lefferts A. Loetscher, eds., *American Christianity* (New York: Scribner, 1963), II, p. 445.

[5] Will Herberg, "Religion and Culture in Present-Day America," in Thomas T. McAvoy, C.S.C., ed., *Roman Catholicism and the American Way of Life* (Notre Dame, Ind.: University of Notre Dame Press, 1960), p. 15. When authors like Niebuhr and Herberg speak of nationalism or the American Way of Life as having become a "religion," they do not stop to define what they mean by "religion." But the reader can infer, in the context, that they mean nationalism has become a religion insofar as it is regarded by its adherents as having a transcendental reference and providing ultimate meaning for man, as does religion in the traditional sense.

[6] *Ibid.*

[7] Carlton J. H. Hayes, *Nationalism: a Religion* (New York: Macmillan, 1960), p. 180.

[8] Daniel Bell, ed., *The New American Right* (New York: Criterion Books, 1955).

[9] Richard Hofstadter, *Anti-Intellectualism in American Life* (New York: Knopf, 1963), p. 136.

[10] Henry J. Browne, "Catholicism in the United States," in James Ward Smith and A. Leland Jamison, eds., *The Shaping of American Religion*, vol. I of *Religion in American Life* (Princeton, N.J.: Princeton University Press, 1961), pp. 72–121.

[11] It can be argued that even the work which is the apparent exception, namely, the novel *The Foundling* (New York: Scribner, 1951), also reflects Cardinal Spellman's nationalism. The two heroes of the book are made to reach their fulfillment by being severely incapacitated from fighting in America's wars.

[12] Louis Schneider and Sanford Dornsbusch, *Popular Religion: Inspirational Books in America* (Chicago: University of Chicago Press, 1958), p. 45.

[13] Karl W. Deutsch, *Nationalism and Social Communication* (Boston: M.I.T. Press, 1953), pp. 3–14.

[14] Martin Buber, *Kampf um Israel Reden und Schriften* (1921–1932) in Salo Wittmayer Baron, *Modern Nationalism and Religion* (New York: Meridian Books, 1960), p. 7.

[15] Boyd C. Shafer, *Nationalism: Interpreters and Interpretations* (2nd ed., Washington, D.C.: Service Center for Teachers of History, 1963), p. 1.

[16] *Ibid.*, p. 2.

[17] Hans W. Gerth and C. Wright Mills, *Character and Social Structure* (New York: Harcourt, Brace, 1954), p. 199.

[18] K. H. Silvert, ed., *Expectant Peoples: Nationalism and Development* (New York: Random House, 1963), p. 19.

[19] *Loc. cit.*

[20] It should be pointed out that nationalism should not be confused with the common-value system. They are distinct concepts and, analytically, they should be treated as such, even though existentially they are intertwined. In practice, as will be indicated in the course of this book, nationalism, the common values of the nation, and the religion which serves at the same time to support nationalism and bolster these common values exist together.

[21] Alexis de Tocqueville, *Democracy in America* (New York: Knopf, 1945), I, p. 393.

[22] *Ibid.*, I, p. 41.

[23] *Ibid.*, I, p. 44: "Liberty regards religion as its companion in all its battles and its triumphs, as the cradle of its infancy and the divine source of its claims. It considers religion as the safeguard of morality and morality as the best security of law and the surest pledge of the duration of freedom." This passage is a particularly pithy summary of the social functions of religion.

[24] Eisenhower, in his 1955 address launching the American Legion's "Back to God" campaign, declared that "Recognition of the Supreme Being is the first, the most basic, expression of Americanism." (From *Protestant-Catholic-Jew* by Will Herberg, p. 258. Copyright © 1955, 1960 by Will Herberg. Reprinted by permission of Doubleday & Company, Inc.

Anthony Trollope remarked on a visit to the United States, made in 1860, that in America "Everybody is bound to have a religion, but it does not matter what it is."

# 2/Religion and Nationalism Among "His Almost Chosen People"[1]

*And we Americans are peculiar, chosen people, the Israel of our times; we bear the ark of the liberties of the world.*—HERMAN MELVILLE

The concept of being a chosen people, a nation blessed uniquely by God, and destined to exercise an exalted mission in behalf of the rest of mankind, is not, of course, exclusive to the citizens of the United States of America. This sense of destiny which accompanies nationalism is of common occurrence throughout the world. But, while many other nations have acquired a sense of national mission in the course of their history, we were born with it.[2]

Like Israel of old, we were a messianic nation from our birth. The Declaration of Independence and our Constitution defined the mission. We were born to exemplify the virtues of democracy and to extend the frontiers of the principles of self-government throughout the world.[3]

The peculiar mixture of religiosity and patriotism which Tocqueville noted, and the strength and persistence of tradi-

12

tional religion in the face of common adherence to the overarching "religion" of the American Way of Life, which Herberg observed, have to be seen in historical perspective to be understood. Even then, it would seem, understanding is only partial. To explain the interaction of American nationalism and religion, the interplay of American democratic values and religious values, the tolerance of different religions and the extreme intolerance of irreligion would be to explain simultaneously the genesis of American nationalism and the shaping of American Christianity. It would mean, moreover, that satisfactory answers had been found to two major questions: Why is the United States so religious (while, at the same time, it is so secular), and why do we have religious pluralism in America? The more one probes for adequate answers to these questions, the more elusive they become. And yet, they cannot be avoided.

To explain the beginnings of nationalism and religion in America demands the successful fitting together of an exceedingly difficult jigsaw puzzle whose pieces are almost all monochromatic. A salutary warning to the person confronting this jigsaw puzzle of events can be taken from the words of Sidney Mead:

. . . Many of them seem to fit into more than one context, others fail to fit nicely into any rational scheme at all. There is no generalization about religious developments in America that cannot be followed by a valid "yes, but" based on an outcast fact. It is a field wherein a measure of ignorance of such facts may be bliss indeed, enabling the interpreter to formulate clear and bold generalizations. By the same token, it is a fearfully baffling field to anyone whose disciplined drive to achieve clarity is balanced by an equally strong aversion to oversimplification. A. N. Whitehead's phrase makes an appropriate motto for the historian of religion in America: "Seek simplicity and distrust it."[4]

On the one hand, there is apparently no agreement among historians about how the puzzle pieces can be fitted together, without forcing them, in order to give a coherent picture of the genesis of religion and nationalism in America;[5] on the other hand, there seems to be no great disagreement about the fact of an American sense of mission. From the days of the earliest settlers, Americans have hoped to achieve a dream of a millennial existence in accord with what they considered their providential destiny.

. . . And from the time of the Puritans, who hoped to achieve "a new heaven and a new earth" in Massachusetts, down to the present day, this dream has been particularly associated with the American continent. The belief that America has a peculiar mission to establish a new and higher way of life has, in fact, become a part of the American character, even though few Americans have been prepared to interpret it in any very radical fashion. It was not religious mystics or radical agitators but sober political leaders who placed on the Great Seal of the United States the words "Novus Ordo Seclorum."[6]

THE MISSION OF AMERICA

Indeed, throughout American history, no matter how much thinkers, religious leaders and statesmen may have differed otherwise, they were in agreement in viewing America as the Promised Land. Ralph Waldo Emerson, Robert C. Ingersoll, Carl Schurz, and David Starr Gordon alike "considered this continent so richly adorned with natural advantages that God must have reserved it for His Chosen People. It was a Land of Canaan meant only for the Children of Israel . . . Even the very remoteness of the country has enabled it to develop this role uncorrupted by the influence of effete people."[7]

Theodore Parker went a step farther in developing the mission of America. Not only was it a Promised Land, but here in America the promise of Christianity was to reach its fruition. Parker felt that only in America could the doctrine of the sacredness of men, germinated in the bosom of the early Christian, come to fruition; for here a new nation "could develop the idea into institutions, and ultimately found an empire on the proposition that *all men are created equal. . . .*"[8]

Documentation of the concept of the United States of America as a destined nation with a sacred mission, as it manifested itself in different epochs of American history, has been extensive. But what is included in this concept? Edward McNall Burns provides a comprehensive answer:

. . . we discover that the following have been considered as the basic elements constituting our myth of purpose and destiny:
First: It is our duty to proclaim liberty throughout the world . . . We must even strive on occasion to extend the blessings of liberty to people less fortunate than we. . . .
Second: The glory of America is to set an example of equality to all nations. . . .
Third: America is the home of the truest and most complete democracy to be found in the world . . . God preserved the American continent from discovery until sufficient progress had been made in Europe to enable the beginnings to be brought to final perfection across the sea. . . .
Fourth: America is the most peaceful and nonmilitaristic of the leading nations . . . When they [Americans] have found it necessary to fight, they have gone into battle armed not merely with swords and guns but with breastplates of righteousness and shields of justice. . . .
Fifth: America is the exemplar of the highest standard of living the world has ever known . . . Americans therefore have a call to confer such blessings [comfort and luxury] upon the rest of mankind.[9]

Elsewhere Burns has commented:

Americans have devoted much time and energy to rationalization of their idea of mission. And the most impressive result is the degree of unanimity that has prevailed among their more active spokesmen. This has been notably true with regard to the assumption of special attributes of the American character. Nearly every speaker and writer, whether liberal or conservative, has assigned the credit for our national superiority to such qualities as initiative, independence, perseverance, industry, frugality, and enterprise. That a nation might experience a call to greatness for its generosity, humanity, tolerance, or justice seems never to have crossed their minds. Though America is officially proclaimed a Christian nation, it is not the virtues of Christianity that are credited with making her great. It is the ethics of the Book of Proverbs and of the Book of Kings and Chronicles that is exalted above all others.[10]

It is not, of course, surprising that the American God-given mission, as well as the American character, should be so marked by an Old Testament flavor when one considers the nature of the Christianity brought to New England shores by the Puritan adapters of Calvinism. As Reinhold Niebuhr points out, however:

It is particularly remarkable that the two great religious-moral traditions which informed our early life—New England Calvinism and Virginian Deism and Jeffersonianism—arrive at remarkably similar conclusions about the meaning of our national character and destiny. Calvinism may have held too pessimistic views of human nature, and too mechanical views of the providential ordering of human life. But when it assessed the significance of the American experiment, both its conceptions of American destiny and its appreciation of American virtue finally arrived at conclusions strikingly similar to those of Deism. Whether our nation interprets its spiritual heritage through Massachusetts or Virginia, we came into existence with the sense of being a "separated" nation, which God was using to make a new beginning for mankind.[11]

While the New England theocrats may have thought primarily of the creation of a new and purer Church, and while Jefferson and his followers aimed primarily to create a new political community, their ideas converged in the belief that Americans had been elected by God to create a new humanity.

## PURITANISM AND RATIONALISM: CONVERGENCE IN EARLY AMERICA

In *Wonder Working Providence of Zion's Saviour* (1650), Edward Johnson expressed the belief that "Jesus Christ had manifested his kingly office toward his churches more fully than ever yet the sons of men saw." However, while Johnson, like other Puritans, emphasized the purity of the church, he envisaged a new and perfect society. Thus he spoke of New England as the place "where the Lord would create a new heaven and a new earth, new churches and a new commonwealth together."[12] John Winthrop had first expressed this millennarian impulse of New England Puritanism when he noted that their colony was like a "city set upon a hill" to establish a pattern for all mankind to follow.[13] This sense of being a chosen people is revealed in the sermons preached in colonial New England. Again and again, preachers "compared the early Jews and the Americans: He had led both out of bondage into freedom; He had shown special mercy and favor to the one as to the other."[14] This special protection was seen as including divine intervention to protect the Puritans from their enemies. Thus, Thomas Shepard, who is called one of the most saintly of the New England ministers, is quoted as describing how, during the Pequod War, "the Providence of God" guided three or four hundreds of the Indians to a place convenient for "the divine slaughter by the hand of the English." Some were put to the sword and some were burned to death when their wigwams were set afire, "until the Lord had utterly consumed the whole company. . . ."[15]

At the time of the Great Awakening in the eighteenth century, the famed New England preacher Jonathan Edwards was proclaiming that the millennium was "probably to begin in America,"[16] and it is plausible, at least, that the notion that this nation was to be the seat of Christ's earthly power enkindled enthusiasm for revolution and independence. At any rate, by the time of the Jeffersonian poet, Freneau (who, incidentally, had rejected orthodox faith), the wedding of the biblical symbolism of the Puritans with the political fervor of the Virginia Deists had given birth to the sentiments expressed in his poem:

> Here independent power shall hold sway
> And public virtue warm the patriot's breast.
> No traces shall remain of tyranny
> And laws and patterns for the world beside
> Be here enacted first.
> A new Jerusalem sent down from heaven
> Shall grace our happy earth.[17]

Jefferson, for his own part, proposed for the seal of the United States a picture of "the children of Israel, led by a cloud by day and a pillar of fire by night." If, at other times in his writings, he did not use biblical imagery, he was nonetheless always aware of the unique character of the people whom he was helping to form into a nation. He declared:

If all the sovereigns of Europe were to set themselves to work to emancipate the minds of their subjects from their present ignorance and prejudice, and that as zealously as they now attempt the contrary, a thousand years would not place them on that high ground on which our common people are now setting out.[18]

In evident agreement with these sentiments concerning the unique character of Americans was Crevecoeur, a young French nobleman. In the 1770's he wrote the series of essays known as *Letters from an American Farmer*. Calling America the "most perfect society now existing in the world," he wrote that "here we have in some measure regained the ancient dignity of our species."[19] Soon after the advent of American nationhood, Parson Weems wrote with evident gusto of America's great destiny: "Perhaps God may be about to establish here a mighty empire, for the reception of a happiness unknown on earth, since the days of blissful Eden."[20]

James Madison's tone is more sober, but his sense of American mission is no less acute than Weems':

The free system of government we have established is so congenial with reason, with common sense, and with a universal feeling, that it must produce approbation and a desire of imitation, as avenues may be found for truth to the knowledge of nations. Our Country, if it does justice to itself, will be the workshop of liberty to the Civilized World, and do more than any other for the uncivilized.[21]

Washington summed up the young nation's sense of destiny by declaring that "The preservation of the sacred fire of liberty and the destiny of the republican model of government are justly considered, perhaps as deeply, as finally staked on the experiment intrusted to the hands of the American people."[22] And John Adams expressed himself even more extravagantly in a letter to Thomas Jefferson: "Many hundred years must roll away before we shall be corrupted. Our pure, virtuous, public-spirited, federative republic will last forever, govern the globe and introduce the perfection of man."[23]

## THE SENSE OF MISSION DEVELOPS

Upon his inauguration, March 4, 1813, James Monroe told his audience:

Never did a government commence under auspices so favorable, nor ever was success so complete. If we look to the history of other nations, ancient and modern, we find no example of a growth so rapid, so gigantic, of a people so prosperous and happy . . . If we persevere in the career in which we have advanced so far and in the path already traced, we cannot fail, under the favor of a gracious Providence, to attain the high destiny which seems to await us.[24]

In not a few of the presidential inaugural addresses similar sentiments are expressed. (It is important to note that it is not always possible to distinguish, on these great national occasions, what are simple expressions of patriotic sentiments —even if somewhat extravagantly expressed—and what are firmly-held commitments to the idea of America as a pre-destined nation with a special mission.) Thus James Buchanan expressed "an humble confidence that the kind Providence which inspired our fathers with wisdom to frame the most perfect form of government and union ever devised by man will not suffer it to perish until it shall have been peacefully instrumental by its example in the extension of civil and religious liberty throughout the world."[25]

Evidently, however, it was not only presidents of the United States, but also ordinary citizens who subscribed to the idea of America's unique blessings. After he had suffered, apparently, from an excess of exposure to this conception, Tocqueville grumbled:

If I say to an American that the country he lives in is a fine one, aye he replies and there is not its equal in the world. If I applaud the freedom its inhabitants enjoy he answers "freedom is a fine thing but few nations are worthy of it." If I remark on the purity of morals that distinguishes the United States he declares "I can imagine that a stranger who has witnessed the corruption which prevails in other nations would be astonished at the difference." At length I leave him to a contemplation of himself. But he returns to the charge and does not desist until he has got me to repeat all I have been saying. It is impossible to conceive of a more troublesome and garrulous patriotism.[26]

Some evidence that Tocqueville had basis for his complaint is found in what Kohn calls "the flamboyant nationalism" of John Louis O'Sullivan, whose article, "The Great Nation of Futurity," was published in November 1839. O'Sullivan wrote:

The expansive future is our arena . . . We are the nation of human progress, and who will, what can, set limits to our onward progress? Providence is with us, and no earthly powers can. We point to the everlasting truths on the first page of our national declaration, and we proclaim to the millions of other lands that the gates of hell—the powers of aristocracy and monarchy—shall not prevail against it. . . . In its magnificent domain of space and time, the nation of many nations is destined to manifest to mankind the excellence of divine principles. . . . For this blessed mission to the nations of the world, which are shut out from the life-giving light of truth, has America been chosen. . . .[27]

Now it is one facet or other of the American system that is hailed. Sometimes it is the American system as a whole that is praised as unique. Thus, Daniel Webster, contemplating the prosperity that the American system has vouchsafed to the country, was moved to pronounce it "a Divine interposition on our behalf,"[28] while Wendell Phillips, extolling the virtue of American democracy, told the Massachusetts Anti-Slavery Society in 1852: "The people never err. The voice of the people is the voice of God."[29]

Lincoln eloquently interpreted the coming of the Civil War as a contest which would decide whether "we would meanly lose or nobly save the last best hope of earth."[30] In 1864, Horace Bushnell moralized about the war:

We associate God and religion with all that we are fighting for . . . Our cause, we love to think, is especially God's and so we are connecting all most sacred impressions with our government itself, weaving in a woof of holy feeling among all the fibres of our constitutional polity and government. . . . The whole shaping of the fabric is Providential. God, God is in it, everywhere . . . every drum-beat is a hymn, the cannon thunder God, the electric silence, darting victory along the wires, is the inaudible greeting of God's favoring work and purpose.[31]

Apparently it was after the Civil War that Americans commenced to extoll their nation's blessed mission in war as they formerly had extolled the blessings that were hers—and which she would bring to the rest of the world—in peace.[32] William E. Channing wrote:

A nation in declaring war should be lifted above its passions by the fearfulness and solemnity of the act. It should appeal with unfeigned confidence to heaven and earth for its uprightness of purpose. It should go forth as the champion of truth and justice, as the minister of God, to vindicate and sustain that great moral and national law, without which life has no security, and social improvements no defence.[33]

While it was not clearly until the Spanish-American War that Americans turned to a consideration of their mission on behalf of distant parts of the world, as early as 1885, Rev. Josiah Strong, describing "the matchless blessings which American expansion would bring to the benighted natives of distant regions, wrote, 'A Christian civilization performs the miracle of the loaves and fishes and feeds its thousands in a desert.' "[34]

## THE AGE OF AMERICA'S MANIFEST DESTINY[35]

"It has been a splendid little war [with Spain]; begun with the highest motives, carried on with magnificent intelligence and spirit, favored by that fortune which loves the brave,"[36] commented John Hay in 1898.

"The splendid little war" manifested to the rest of the world America's sense of destiny. True, certain Americans, like Senator Hoar of Massachusetts, condemned our imperialistic ambitions, avowing that our founding fathers "would have never betrayed these sacred and awful verities that they might strut about in the cast-off clothing of emperors and pewter kings."[37] But their voices were drowned out by such men as Theodore Roosevelt who "believed that war released or evoked the manly virtues without which the individual did not truly experience life and without which no country could remain a vigorous organism,"[38] and who saw in the Spanish-American War an opportunity to assure ourselves that the power and vitality of the nation were not waning. Albert Beveridge, on September 16, 1898, before President McKinley had decided to keep the Philippines, delivered himself of the following sentiments:

Think of the thousands of Americans who will pour into Hawaii and Porto Rico when the republic's laws cover those islands with justice and safety. Think of the tens of thousands of Americans who will invade mine and forest and field in the Philippines when a liberal government, protected and controlled by this republic, if not the government of the republic itself, shall establish order and equity there! Think of the hundreds of thousands of Americans who will build a soap-and-water, common-school civilization of energy and industry in Cuba, when a government of law replaces the double reign of anarchy and tyranny!—think of the prosperous millions that Empress of Islands will support when, obedient to the law of political gravitation, her people ask for the highest honor liberty can bestow, the sacred Order of her Stars and Stripes, the citizenship of the Great Republic![39]

After his election to the Senate, Beveridge expressed himself even more bluntly. Discussing the conquest of the Philippines, he noted that we did not "renounce our part in the mission of our race, trustee under God of the civilization of the world." God, in appointing English-speaking and Teutonic people to a higher calling, "had made them adepts in government in order that they might establish system where chaos reigns" and administer the affairs of "savage and senile people."[40]

For a while, McKinley, on his part, evidently did not see as clearly as Beveridge that the Philippines had to be kept as part of America's destiny, for, as he told a group of fellow Methodists, he sought divine guidance,

And one night late it came to me this way . . . that there was nothing left for us to do but to take them all, and to educate the Filipinos, and uplift them and civilize and Christianize them and by God's grace do the very best we could by them, as our fellow men, for whom Christ died.[41]

Possibly the greatest theorist to elucidate America's destiny in war was Alfred T. Mahan, Theodore Roosevelt's mentor. Burns remarks that, in Mahan's opinion,

Christianity was an essential factor not only in developing in nations the capacity for self-government but in making them fit to govern. . . . As long as evil exists in the world, it will be justifiable to use force to combat it. For this reason the great literary sea dog opposed the signing of treaties which would require America to arbitrate her disputes with other countries. The nation must be free to obey the higher law of God which invalidates any statute or agreement of men involving a concession to unrighteousness.[42]

For Mahan, force was "a faculty of national life; one of the talents committed to nations by God."[43] Here he was in agreement with Senator Beveridge who pronounced the American people "a conquering race who must obey their blood and occupy new markets and, if necessary, new lands. God had ordained it so. He had made it a part of His infinite plan."[44]

## DEEPER INTO DESTINY

Niebuhr and Heimert remark that "One of the moral hazards of a democracy, particularly one with a strong sense of mission, is that it cannot engage in wars, except they be for 'righteousness' sake,' real or pretended."[45] They go on to say that "both the President and the nation found a moral purpose in the contest after we entered the war [World War I], though it had eluded our minds before we entered the war."[46] Wilson expressed the belief that there are times when nations must accept the challenge of battle "in order to vindicate spiritual conceptions. For liberty is a spiritual conception and when men take up arms to set other men free, there is something sacred and holy in the warfare."[47] The identification of patriotism with righteousness was the key to Wilson's wartime philosophy. Declaring that America had been given birth by a patriotism, spiritual and unselfish in type, he saw her destiny "to show men the paths of liberty and mutual serviceability."[48]

Evidently an American of the type that Tocqueville had complained about, Wilson could not believe that other countries could also be fired by moral idealism. This distrust was behind his refusal to join the Allies; the United States joined the war instead as an "associated" power.

One could hardly have judged from his [Wilson's] speeches that the Allies knew anything about courage and sacrifice and suffering, or that some of the Allied leaders also had ideas. We Americans, it seemed, were to be freedom's chief, if not first and only champion.[49]

At the end of the war, President Wilson still saw America as a special ward of Providence, and, in his wholehearted commitment to the League of Nations, he warned his country that, if the United States rejected the League, "the vengeful Providence of God" would bring a new war.[50]

The League was rejected, but the national sense of mission did not cease. At his inaugural, March 4, 1921, Warren G. Harding delivered himself of these thoughts:

. . . Mindful of the solemnity of this occasion . . . I must utter my belief in the divine inspiration of the founding fathers. Surely there must have been God's intent in the making of this new-world Republic . . . We have seen the world rivet its hopeful gaze on the great truths on which the founders wrought. We have seen civil, human, and religious liberty verified and glorified. In the beginning the Old World scoffed at our experiment; today our foundations of political and social belief stand unshaken, a precious inheritance to ourselves, an inspiring example of freedom and civilization to all mankind.[51]

Harding's successor, Calvin Coolidge, included the following passage in his inaugural address:

America seeks no earthly empire built on blood and force. No ambitions, no temptations, lures her to thought of foreign dominations. The legions which she sends forth are armed, not with the sword, but with the cross.[52] The higher state to which she seeks the allegiance of all mankind is not of human, but of divine origin. She cherishes no purpose save to merit the favor of Almighty God.[53]

The circumstances of the twentieth century have not changed the fundamental nature of American nationalism. It is still based on the characteristic outlook of the American of the seventeenth and eighteenth centuries. And, as Commager remarked, in the middle of the twentieth century "the American was still optimistic, still took for granted that his was the most favored of all countries, the happiest and most virtuous of all societies, and, though less sure of progress, was still confident that the best was yet to be . . ."[54]

And this American can still declare with William Stoughton (in the words he used shortly after the settlement of New England):

If any people have been lifted up to advantages and privilege, we are the people . . . we have had the eye and hand of God working everywhere for our good. Our adversaries have had their rebukes and we have had our encouragements and a wall of fire around us.[55]

## RELIGION DEFINES OUR SECULAR DESTINY

A messianic nation from our birth, born to cherish and maintain the blessings of liberty and democracy, and imbued with a sense of providential mission on behalf of all mankind, we have kept our idea and ideal of national destiny surprisingly unchanged throughout the years of America's existence, as the words of thinkers and statesmen which have been quoted were intended to show. Moreover, all these quotations, whether or not they are couched in traditional religious terms or give explicit acknowledgement to God as source of American destiny, seem to recognize, at least implicitly, that this destiny is "divine."

There apparently is consensus, not only on a core of values that are at the heart of our national life, but also on the fact that somehow or other (in a way perhaps left vague and ill-defined) religion is intrinsic to that core. If atheism is un-American, it is because throughout our existence as a nation our self-identity as well as our mission have been conceived in religious terms.[56] If it is too much to claim that religion gave birth to the United States of America, it does not seem untrue to single out religion as the midwife at that birth. And, for religion, America consistently claimed respect, acknowledging her part in the nation's safe delivery. As nineteenth-century visitors noted repeatedly, Americans tolerated different religions, but have always been manifestly intolerant to irreligion, as if to deny religion were somehow or other to deny the facts of the nation's birth, as well as to imperil her continued prosperous existence.

The religious basis of American nationalism (in particular, our sense of destiny) is not difficult to explain; the reasons for its persistence may be less comprehensible. The Puritans founded the colonies with a sense of religious mission. This was taken over by rationalists whose secular concept of destiny nevertheless could profitably use the tradition and support of religion. Paradoxically, the political ideas of the Enlightenment found in the sense of American mission, originally supplied by religion, a source not only of great strength, but also, and more importantly, of their legitimation.[57] Religion could have this effect since men of the Enlightenment, like Franklin and Jefferson—showing themselves as aware as any modern functionalist of the social consequences of religion, particularly "to preserve peace and order"[58]—were willing to ally their thought with religious tradition. They looked to the churches or sects to "inculcate the basic religious beliefs essential for the existence and well-being of the society,"[59] and thus to support the new nation whose political foundations they were in the process of laying.

In observing the convergence of the Puritan tradition and the ideas of the Enlightenment in forming the basis for American nationalism, it is striking to note how gracefully the union was accomplished. This was no mismating of minds, but a ready consensus. In the convergence of the religious with the political ideas of destiny and of mission, of freedom and of individual worth, did the United States find at the time of its inception that "*common* religion" which Robin Williams contends is necessary "for every functioning society"? Flowing from this—and stating it boldly—could the United States allow pluralism in religion because in many important respects it already had a *common* religion? In other words, could the United States afford to reject the notion of religious establishment, and thus the common cognitive orientations, expressive meanings, and common rituals and symbols heretofore provided in a society by a common religion (in the traditional sense), because it already had for that common religion an adequate substitute? We shall return to this thought in a later chapter.

The causes of religious pluralism in America have been hotly debated. Some authors account for it on reasons of expediency or pragmatism. Thus Daniel D. Williams sees religious pluralism and, more directly, the rejection of religious establishment as "derived partly from the need for freedom of sectarian religious groups . . . and partly from the insights of rationalists, deists and free thinkers that no establishment was possible without creating hopeless divisions in the body politic."[60]

To agree with Williams is not the same as to disagree with the idea that, in America, a consensus had already been established; indeed, it may be that, because there was already agreement about the ultimate values and the ultimate meaning of the American nation, such expediency in the matter of religious disestablishment was possible.

## THE REASONS BEHIND RELIGIOUS PLURALISM

Sidney Mead, for one, disagrees with those who maintain that the original Protestantism which was brought to America held the idea of religious liberty which harmonized so well with the ideas of freedom of the Enlightenment. He argues for his own position that the original Protestant settlers, in fact, "agreed with Roman Catholics on the necessity for enforcing religious uniformity in doctrine and practice within a civil commonwealth. This view of many centuries' standing in Christendom the new churches accepted without question."[61] And yet, "The tradition of thirteen-centuries' standing was given up in the relatively brief time of one hundred and eighty years."[62]

How, then, does Mead account for the coming of religious pluralism?

Accepting, then, the view that the original intention of the dominant and really powerful groups was to perpetuate the patterns of religious uniformity, I shall argue that this intention was frustrated by the unusual problems posed by the vast space with which the Planters had to deal, by a complex web of self-interest in which they were enmeshed, and by the practical necessity to connive at religious variety which both space and self-interest imposed. Finally, too, pressures from the motherland contributed to the process leading to religious freedom.[63]

The English colonists, encircled by Spanish and French Catholic colonies, could not afford the luxury of exacting uniformity of religious beliefs from those fellow Protestants whom they induced to join them in settlement. Furthermore, where such uniformity was required, it soon proved itself impractical to enforce. Dissenters could always move on (from Massachusetts Bay Colony to Rhode Island, because of the "great space" Mead emphasizes), and, after awhile, such movement was unnecessary, since even the knowledge that dissent existed elsewhere soon made dissent permissible where formerly uniformity prevailed. Distance also allowed religious divergence to grow, free from any effective ecclesiastical control. And when, in 1663, the Crown, "in giving its consent to Rhode Island's 'lively experiment' with 'full liberty in religious concernments,' in the new Charter, gave official sanction to the scandal of Massachusetts Bay and forestalled all future attempts on the part of the Bay Puritans to impose their kind of theocratic order,"[64] it was taking one of many steps that worked for the broadening of colonial toleration. But, according to Mead, the propelling energy behind the final thrust for religious freedom came from the coalition of pietistic revivalists and the rationalists. If the latter provided the *rationale* for religious toleration,[65] the former provided the *heart* for it. For the pietists, in revolt against the restraints of the traditionalists in the churches, were concerned that the spiritually hungry "could not find nourishment in formal creeds, massive theologies, or bare intellectual propositions." Instead, they sought to find peace and a basis for unity in personal spiritual experience.

The rationalists appealed to the head, and concluded that all the multifarious differences over which Christian churchmen fought were matters of nonessential opinion. At the same time pietists appealed to the heart and concluded that the differences over which Christians had battled and bled for a millennium were immaterial between those of like heart.[66]

While rationalists and pietists represented different religious outlooks, they reached the same conclusion: both groups opted for religious freedom.[67]

Their consensus was not a transitory phenomenon; in fact, so intertwined had become the secular and the religious idea of freedom in the ultimate ideology of Americans that Tocqueville could write half a century after the foundation of the United States: "The Americans combine the notions of Christianity and of liberty so intimately in their minds that it is impossible to make them conceive the one without the other . . ."[68]

"In France I had always seen the spirit of religion and the spirit of freedom marching in opposite directions. But in America I found they were intimately united and that they reigned in common over the same country."[69] No matter how great a part expediency had in the creation of a system of pluralism, by the time that system came into being so permanently intertwined were religious values with the political value of liberty that, for the American, they seemed to be incapable of existing, one without the other. To have answered the question—Why is there religious pluralism in America? —is to have answered the initial question—Why is America so religious? It is to religion that the American nation has continued to look to corroborate and to confirm its identity, to support it in its pursuit of its destiny; for it is religion which gives sanction and support to America's democratic mission.

BENJAMIN FRANKLIN: A CASE IN POINT

But perhaps the ultimate values of America betray the element of expediency in their ancestry. At least, such is the thought provoked by Tocqueville's remarking that American preachers always had to prove to their congregations the utility of religion.[70] This stress on the practical uses of religion has evidently persisted. Thus, in a book written to explain American culture to a mass audience, Bradford Smith writes:

> Because it has been important to us not to let religion interfere with our national unity, we have stressed the unifying nature of faith rather than the disuniting effects of many faiths. . . .
> As in all things, so in religion, too, the American wants to see results. If religion makes men better, if it leads them to good works, good thoughts and good conduct, then it deserves to be supported. Religion has to deliver the goods. It has to contribute to morality, peace and order, even to individual success, and it does.
> . . . The influence of religion is thus to reinforce American optimism and perfectionism.[71]

These words show the surprising persistence of that attitude toward religion as reinforcement of American values which has evidently continued since our nation's beginnings. Indeed, the passage from Bradford Smith could have been written by Benjamin Franklin who in his writings reflects the marriage of the Protestant tradition with rationalism.[72] Convinced of the utility of religion in preserving the peace and order of the commonwealth, Franklin declared that he "regularly paid my annual subscription for the support of the only Presbyterian minister or meeting we had," and he urged his daughter to "go constantly to church, whoever preaches."[73] Mead remarks of men like Franklin, "whose primary interest was in good citizens, and who could see that even the worst sects 'had

some good effects' in producing them," that they were prepared to note that "all sects were good enough."[74]

Asked by Ezra Stiles about his belief in the divinity of
Christ, Franklin showed what seems to have become the characteristic American indifference to the substance of faith
(noted by Bradford Smith). He replied:

I have, with most of the Dissenters in England, some Doubts as
to his Divinity; tho' it is a question I do not dogmatize upon,
having never studied it, and [this was a month before his death]
think it needless to busy myself with it now, when I expect an
Opportunity of knowing the Truth with less Trouble.

And he added—with a characteristic feeling for the utility
of faith—

I see no harm . . . in its being believed, if that Belief has good
Consequence, as probably it has, of making his Doctrines more
respected and better observed. . . .[75]

For Franklin, however, everything was really irrelevant in
religion which he considered irrelevant for the general welfare
of the nation-community. Thus he rejected a minister whose
sermons seemed aimed "rather to make us Presbyterians than
good citizens."[76] There is no doubt that Franklin would have
agreed that the condition of American religion (as later it
was observed by Tocqueville) was to be commended:

Each sect adores the Deity in its own peculiar manner, but all sects
preach the same moral law in the name of God . . . Society has
no future life to hope for or to fear; and provided the citizens profess a religion, the peculiar tenets of that religion are of little
importance to its interests.[77]

For, despite the fact that the intellectual and theological
elements of religion had been important to his American

Protestant ancestors, Franklin himself (and evidently a good number of his fellow Americans) saw the important element of religion as being the moral.[78] Concerned with the effect of religion on the individual's conduct and on the well-being of the community, he seems to have already attained to that tremendous unconcern for the transcendent meaning of religion which Herberg decries in contemporary Americans. Franklin's religion was secular in that it had no meaning apart from its worldly utility.

What can be discerned in the writings of Franklin is a religious aura with scant religious belief. This is, in fact, what Max Weber notes in his classic *The Protestant Ethic and the Spirit of Capitalism,* when he uses Franklin as the exemplar of the spirit of mature capitalism which has become an end in itself, independent of the Calvinist ethos which originally motivated it. For Franklin, "time is money." And "Without industry and frugality nothing will do, and with them every thing." But this is so for utilitarian and pecuniary motivation. These virtues are preached with a religious seriousness, but without religious motivation. In Franklin one notes none of the feeling of worthlessness or sense of inherent evil in the self of the early settlers. It would seem that, while he assumed his own election and that of his fellow citizens, it was not (as it was for the earlier Calvinists) because their prosperity had become a sign of the free choice of God, in spite of their sinfulness. Rather, Franklin seemed to assume the worthiness of all concerned; for Franklin, like Jefferson (who saw our ordinary people as being a thousand years ahead of the Europeans), Americans are not only chosen, but worthy of the choice of Providence.

While Franklin, in his writings and his conduct, continued to extoll the life of the "inner-worldly ascetic,"[79] the virtues of this life had become the support of good citizenship and

American democratic goals. By the time of Franklin, the stage was set for that peculiar union of nationalism and religiosity that has been characteristically American.

. . . Democratic and religious values have grown together. The results have been that, on the one hand, Americans see religion as essential to the support of the democratic institutions they cherish, and therefore feel that all Americans should profess some sort of religious faith; on the other hand, American denominations stress the ethical side of religion which they all have in common (and which is closely associated with other democratic values) rather than stressing transcendental beliefs wherein they differ. At the same time, democracy, by giving religious institutions a specific role in American society, has allowed them to proliferate, to adjust to peculiar needs, and to have a limited influence on their members' lives.[80]

It is against this background of the interaction of American democratic and religious values that the issue of nationalism in American Catholicism has to be viewed. What was the response of immigrant Catholics (particularly the hierarchy) as they confronted the particular American form of national messianism? Did they find any difficulty in conforming to national goals or in identifying themselves with American symbol and ritual? Have they been aware, over the years, of any dilemmas between "the altar and the flag"?

These are some of the questions which will next be considered.

## NOTES

[1] Bruce Catton, in "The Unfinished Business of the Civil War," *The New York Times Magazine*, April 4, 1965, pp. 28–29, quotes Lincoln addressing the New Jersey Senate in the winter of 1861 as expressing

the hope that he himself might become an instrument in the hands of the Almighty "and of this, His almost chosen people . . ."

[2] Hans Kohn, *American Nationalism: An Interpretative Essay* (New York: Macmillan, 1957), p. 13: "In its very origin as a nation the United States was the embodiment of an idea. As Professor Richard Hofstadter has put it felicitously, 'It has been our fate as a nation, not to have ideologies but to be one.' "

[3] Reinhold Niebuhr and Alan Heimert, *A Nation So Conceived* (New York: Scribner, 1963), p. 123.

[4] From *The Lively Experiment*, pp. x–xi, Sidney E. Mead, copyrighted 1963 by the author, used by permission of Harper & Row, Publishers, Inc., New York.

[5] Kohn, for example, in *American Nationalism*, sees religion as being formed by American values, whereas Mead, *op. cit.*, seems to stress rather the influence of religion on American secular values.

[6] Henry Bamford Parkes, *The American Experience: An Interpretation of the History and Civilization of the American People* (2nd ed. rev.; New York: Knopf, 1955), p. 78.

[7] Edward McNall Burns, *The American Idea of Mission* (New Brunswick, N.J.: Rutgers Univ. Press, 1957), p. 62. "It is important to note, however, that not all Americans who subscribed to the notion of America as a Promised Land did so in the same way. For some, this notion implied uncritical acceptance of American national goals; for others (such as Emerson), condemnation of the chauvinistic type of national loyalty was combined with the healthy realization that every other country likewise believed that the Divine Providence had a sneaking kindness for it?' " Ralph Waldo Emerson, *Journals* (Boston and New York, 1909–1914), X, p. 195, as quoted in Merle Curti, *The Roots of American Loyalty* (New York: Columbia Univ. Press, 1946), p. 202.

[8] Theodore Parker, *Writings* (Centenary ed.; Boston: American Unitarian Assoc., 1907–1916), VIII, p. 281, as quoted in Burns, *op. cit.*

[9] Burns, *op. cit.*, p. 348. Compare these points with those included in the speeches of one of the most outspoken heralds of American manifest destiny, Albert Jeremiah Beveridge. Hans Kohn lists them as: "geopolitical concepts of providentially shaped geographic or continental limits; the conviction of the superior ability and morality of the Americans; the excellence of democracy and its universal mission to extend this blessing; the advanced stage of the American economy

and technology which would make the desert bloom . . ." (*American Nationalism*, p. 194).

[10] Burns, *op. cit.*, pp. 56–57.

[11] Reinhold Niebuhr, *The Irony of American History* (New York: Scribner, 1952), p. 24.

[12] *Ibid.*, p. 25.

[13] Niebuhr and Heimert, *op. cit.*, p. 125.

[14] Curti, *op. cit.*, p. 67. Curti indicates that not only New England preachers, but ministers in the other colonies as well, developed the notion of Americans as a chosen people, both before and after the Revolutionary War. Thus, Isaac Keith of Charleston declared in 1789 that "The citizens of the United States are the object of divine providential care."

[15] Alexander Young, *Chronicles of the First Planters of the Colony of Massachusetts Bay* (1846), pp. 549, 550, as quoted by Parkes, *op. cit.*, p. 68.

[16] Jonathan Edwards, *Some Thoughts Concerning the Present Revival of Religion in New England*, as quoted by Niebuhr and Heimert, *op. cit.*, p. 125.

[17] Niebuhr, *op. cit.*, p. 125.

[18] *Ibid.*, p. 70.

[19] Ralph Barton Perry, *Puritanism and Democracy* (New York: Vanguard, 1944), pp. 585–586.

[20] Mason L. Weems, *A History of the Life and Death, Virtues and Exploits of General George Washington*, p. 75, as quoted by Perry, *op. cit.*, p. 196.

[21] Adrienne Koch, *Power, Morals, and the Founding Fathers* (Ithaca, N.Y.: Cornell Univ. Press, 1961), p. 105.

[22] Washington's First Inaugural Address, *Inaugural Addresses of the Presidents of the United States* (82nd Congress, 2nd Session, House Document no. 540, 1952), p. 3.

[23] Kohn, *American Nationalism*, p. 13.

[24] *Inaugural Addresses*, p. 33.

[25] *Ibid.*, p. 93.

[26] Tocqueville, *Democracy in America*, II, p. 225.

[27] Kohn, *American Nationalism*, p. 182.

[28] Daniel Webster, *The Works of Daniel Webster* (Boston: Little, Brown, 1868), I, p. 404, as quoted in Burns, *op. cit.*, p. 90.

[29] Wendell Phillips, *Complete Prose Works* (Boston: Small, Maynard, 1898), p. 146, as quoted in Burns, *op. cit.*, p. 240.

[30] Mead, *op. cit.*, "Abraham Lincoln's 'Last, Best Hope of Earth'." Mead stresses Lincoln's sense of proportion, however, in his conception of America's—and particularly the North's—mission. He writes (p. 74) of "Lincoln's uncanny knack of putting first things first, as when a certain clergyman wrote him expressing the hope that God was on the side of the North. Lincoln replied that this did not worry him, but that he was concerned that the North be on God's side."

[31] Horace Bushnell, *Popular Government by Divine Right* (Hartford: L. E. Hunt, 1864), as quoted in Mead, *op. cit.*, p. 142.

[32] Kohn, *American Nationalism*, p. 179, remarks that the American attitude toward war was always ambivalent. Americans disliking army life and high brass have always rejected the military ideal venerated by the French and Germans. He sees the origin of this anti-militarist attitude perhaps in the social and evangelistic character of Anglo-American Reformed Christianity. "Yet anti-militarism was in no sense identical with pacifism. It could, at times, lend a note of crusading morality and bellicosity to American involvement in war. Julia Ward Howe's 'Battle Hymn of the Republic' is an outstanding example of this Christian and moralistic battle spirit."

[33] William E. Channing, *The Works of W. E. Channing* (Boston: Amer. Unitarian Assoc., 1877), pp. 662–663, as quoted in Burns, *op. cit.*, p. 239.

[34] Josiah Strong, *Our Country* (New York: Baker and Taylor, 1885), pp. 14–15, as quoted in Burns, *op. cit.*, p. 217.

[35] The term "manifest destiny" had, of course, been used earlier. Thus, John Louis O'Sullivan defended America's claim to Oregon, in his article, "The True Title," as based on the right "of our manifest destiny to overspread and to possess the whole continent which providence has given us . . ." Kohn, *op. cit.*, p. 183.

[36] Thomas A. Bailey, *The American Spirit* (Boston: Heath, 1963), II, p. 590.

[37] Niebuhr and Heimert, *op. cit.*, p. 131.

[38] Curti, *op. cit.*, p. 198. Curti remarks that "Having no doubt that all the wars America had engaged in were righteous, he [Roosevelt] could not envision one which would not be righteous." Roosevelt, moreover, declared on one occasion that he could not understand those who

objected to Stephen Decatur's words: "My country right, my country wrong; but right or wrong, my country."

[39] Bailey, *op. cit.*, II, pp. 609–610.

[40] *Congressional Record*, 56th Congress, 1st Session, XXXIII, pp. 704, 711, 1900, as quoted in Burns, *op. cit.*, p. 218.

[41] *The Christian Advocate*, Jan. 22, 1903, as quoted in Bailey, *op. cit.*, II, p. 606.

McKinley here speaks in the tradition of the sense of divine mission which has been traced back to the Puritan colonists. This belief in America's God-given destiny (which may be viewed as a religious belief expressing itself in nationalistic terms) is radically different from the jingoism of William Randolph Hearst, which was operative at the same time, even though both ideologies expressed themselves and converged in the action of the United States in the Spanish-American War. The two ideological strands continue to be intertwined in American nationalism.

[42] Burns, *op. cit.*, p. 217.

[43] *Ibid.*, p. 249.

[44] *Ibid.*, p. 264.

[45] Niebuhr and Heimert, *op. cit.*, p. 137.

[46] *Ibid.*

[47] Burns, *op. cit.*, p. 247.

[48] *The Public Papers of Woodrow Wilson*, I, p. 437, as quoted by Curti, *op. cit.*, p. 232.

[49] H. C. F. Bell, *Woodrow Wilson and the People* (New York: Doubleday, 1945), as quoted by Kohn, *American Nationalism*, p. 204.

[50] Burns, *op. cit.*, p. 218.

[51] *Inaugural Addresses*, p. 197.

[52] Note that Coolidge, speaking at a time when sentiment was strong against war, differed from his predecessors who could proclaim the sword at the service of the cross. For instance, there is a recording of William Howard Taft, with a plea for missions on one side and an equally strong plea for a stronger Army and Navy on the other side of the record. Tracey K. Jones, Jr., *Our Mission Today: The Beginnings of a New Age* (New York: World Outlook Press, 1963), p. 25.

[53] *Inaugural Addresses*, p. 213.

[54] Henry Steele Commager, *The American Mind: An Interpretation of American Thought and Character since the 1880's* (New Haven: Yale Univ. Press, 1950), p. 409.

[55] William Stoughton (1631–1703), "New England's True Interest," as quoted by Reinhold Niebuhr, *op. cit.*, p. 51.

[56] Tocqueville, *op. cit.*, I, p. 306: "While I was in America, a witness who happened to be called at the Sessions of the County of Chester (State of New York) declared that he did not believe in the existence of God or in the immortality of the soul. The judge refused to admit his evidence, on the ground that the witness had destroyed beforehand all the confidence of the court in what he was about to say."

[57] If religion originally gave legitimation to the values of our democracy, these secular values themselves inevitably influenced the subsequent development of religion in America. It seems apparent that it is the interplay of the two sets of values in our history that has accounted for the pervasiveness of religion in America and its surprising secularity—twin phenomena noted by analysts such as Tocqueville, Herberg, Lipset and Robin Williams.

Commenting on the interplay of religious and democratic values from the beginning of our nation's history, Lipset remarks: "The gradual identification of Enlightenment ideals with national identity in turn affected the content of our religious values. J. Franklin Jameson explains the amazingly rapid decline of Calvinist doctrine in America after the Revolution, and its replacement by Arminian religious beliefs, not only as a reflection of the doctrinal need of evangelistic revivalistic religion, but also by the assumption that, 'in a period when the special privileges of individuals were being called into question or being destroyed, there would naturally be less favor for that form of theology which was dominated by the doctrine of the especial election of a part of mankind, a growing favor for forms which seemed more distinctly to be based upon the idea of the natural equality of all men.' " *The American Revolution Considered as a Social Movement* (Princeton, N.J.: Princeton University Press, 1926), p. 157.

"The Arminian emphasis on the personal attainment of grace, perhaps even more than the Calvinist stress on the existence of an 'elect,' served as a religious parallel to the secular emphasis on equality of opportunity and achievement. This parallelism, and even mutual reinforcement, was noted by many nineteenth-century foreign visitors." —Seymour N. Lipset, *The First New Nation* (New York: Basic Books, 1963), p. 163.

[58] Jefferson, *Notes on the State of Virginia: Written in 1781*, as quoted in Mead, *op. cit.*, p. 59.

[59] Mead, *op. cit.*, p. 65.

[60] "Tradition and Experience," in Smith and Jamison, *Religion in American Life*, p. 475.

[61] Mead, *op. cit.*, p. 16.

[62] *Ibid.*, p. 18.

[63] *Ibid.*, p. 20.

[64] *Ibid.*, p. 26.

[65] Mead comments, p. 36: "Most of the effectively powerful intellectual, social, and political leaders were rationalists, and these men made sense theoretically out of the actual, practical situation which demanded religious freedom. They gave it tangible form and legal structure. This the churches, each intent on its own freedom, accepted in practice but without reconciling themselves to it intellectually by developing theoretical defenses of religious freedom that were legitimately rooted in their professed theological positions. And they never have. Anson Phelps Stokes' massive three-volume work on *Church and State in the United States*, proceeding over the historical evidence like a vacuum cleaner over a rug, is notable for the paucity of positive Protestant pronouncements on religious freedom that it sweeps up."

[66] *Ibid.*, pp. 40–41.

[67] One religious leader who did present reasoned arguments for religious freedom was John Leland, a Baptist minister who wrote against religious establishment in Virginia. "Religion is a matter between God and individuals, religious opinions of men not being the objects of civil government nor in any other way under its control" (H. Shelton Smith, Robert T. Handy, and Lefferts A. Loetscher, *American Christianity: An Historical Interpretation with Representative Documents* [New York, Scribner, 1963] I, p. 470).

"These establishments metamorphose the church into a creature, and religion into a principle of state, with a natural tendency to make men conclude that *bible religion* is nothing but a trick of state" (*Ibid.*, p. 472).

Thus Leland, out of concern for the integrity of biblical religion reached the same conclusion as the rationalists, who—arguing from different premises and for different reasons—opted for disestablishment and complete religious freedom. This convergence of religious adherents and rationalists that civil government had no business involving itself with the regulation or establishment of religion is demonstrated again and again in the course of American history. Thus, Senator Brown of Georgia, in a speech before the U.S. Senate in 1882, spoke against a bill outlawing polygamy (directed against the Mormons), using as his argument the fact that the bill "proposes to apply a religious test to the Mormons"—a power forbidden the federal government by the Bill of Rights. Speaking against this attempt to regulate religion, Brown warned the Senators: "You are treading on dangerous ground when you open this floodgate anew." William Mulder and A. Russell Mortensen, eds., *Among the Mormons* (New York: Knopf, 1958), pp. 408–410.

[68] Tocqueville, *op. cit.*, I, p. 306.

[69] *Ibid.*, I, p. 308.

[70] *Ibid.*, II, pp. 126–127.

[71] From *Why We Behave Like Americans* by Bradford Smith, pp. 111–112. Copyright © 1957 by Bradford Smith. Published by J. B. Lippincott Company.

[72] In his *Autobiography*, Franklin wrote: "I had been religiously educated as a Presbyterian; and tho' some of the dogmas of that persuasion, such as the *eternal decrees of God, election, reprobation,* etc., appeared to me unintelligible, others doubtful, and I early absented myself from the public assemblies of the sect, Sunday being my studying day, I never was without some religious principles. I never doubted, for instance, the existence of the Deity; that he made the world, and govern'd it by his Providence; that the most acceptable service of God was the doing of good to men; that our souls are immortal; and that all crime will be punished, and virtue rewarded, either here or hereafter. These I esteemed the essentials of every religion; and, being to be found in all the religions we had in our country, I respected them all . . . This respect to all, with an opinion that the worst had some good effects, induced me to avoid all discourse that might tend to lessen the good opinion another might have of his own religion; and as our province increas'd in people, and new places of worship were continually wanted . . . my mite for such purpose, whatever might be the sect, was never refused." Mead, *op. cit.*, p. 64.

[73] Mead, *op. cit.*, p. 41.

[74] *Ibid.*, p. 64.

[75] *Ibid.*, p. 45.

[76] *Ibid.*, p. 66.

[77] Tocqueville, *op. cit.*, I, p. 314.

[78] Lipset, following William Lee Miller in Smith and Jamison, *op. cit.*, p. 94, would account for the stress on the moral as the result of the "growth of the churches of the common man and the triumph of pietism." Parkes, *op. cit.*, p. 82, seems to trace it directly to the influence of Jonathan Edwards which inculcated "an American trust in the individual and an American humanitarianism;" with "the drive of the American will toward domination," to replace the original Calvinist theology and its emphasis on the utter sinfulness of man.

[79] Max Weber, *The Sociology of Religion*, trans. by Ephraim Fischoff (Boston: Beacon paperback, 1964), Chapter XI, "Asceticism, Mysticism, and Salvation Religion."

[80] Lipset, *op. cit.*, p. 169.

# 3/Background of Nationalism and American Catholicism

*"I no longer hold my God and my country to be identical"*[1]

American messianism and the use of religion to support American national goals have not always been accepted unthinkingly or uncritically by Americans.[2] This criticism apparently has become especially forthright and cogent in periods (such as after World War I) when so-called one-hundred-per-cent patriotism flourishes and when the merits and rights of people other than Americans, as well as the transcendental claims of religion, are in jeopardy.[3]

Protestant theologians, especially the two Niebuhrs, have written extensively of the dangers of identifying Christ and culture, Christianity and American nationalism.[4] More recently, Martin E. Marty has warned against the syncretism of Christianity with nationalism in America. Warning against the presence among church-going Christians of an integral nationalism (placing their country above everything else) which he sees as a "variety of unbelief," and thus a substitute for genuine religion, Marty writes:

From the viewpoint of Christian belief the problem with nationalism is its capture of the transcendent note, rendering irrelevant

45

the witness to God's action in history outside the immediacy of the nation. Such a religion justifies man as it produces cohesiveness of the pluralist experience.[5]

Elsewhere, Marty notes the functions that traditional religious institutions perform in a society where there is disestablishment:

They may serve to integrate their members when secularity bewilders them. They can provide people with identity and motivation to serve the whole culture. At the same time, it is normally incumbent upon such [religious] institutions to be the most loyal, most patriotic supporters of the civil state. In national crisis they tend to look like the most warlike element, no matter what their peacetime pretensions. They serve to bless the weapons and to denominate each war as "just" or "justified."

When the sense of transcendence was more markedly felt, religious institutions which specialized in witnessing to it could escape into apocalypticism. On the national scale the eschatological note does not prevail in today's America, and the churches have the problems of disestablishing themselves from the roles which society provides them and which they do not always choose.

. . . The perplexing task for historic churches in congenial secular cultures is to carry on positive relations with what is good in the environment and yet to be free to step back and utter a transcendent word . . .[6]

Agreeing with Paul Tillich that "nationalism can produce an ecstasy which few other idolatries can,"[7] Marty yet expresses the hope that America will understand "that a religiously transcendent note can judge the pride of nations. 'The Almighty has his own purposes': 'He that sitteth in the heavens shall laugh.' A free society permits these reminders as a check on nationalism; a totalitarian one does not."[8]

ANOTHER "IRONY OF AMERICAN HISTORY"

Marty notes that the literature on the religious dimensions of nationalism is unanimous on this point: "No other rival to the historic faiths is better organized on a worldwide scale or more acceptable as a parallel religion to adherents of historic faiths."[9] Perhaps it is this acceptability of nationalism which accounts for another—and present—irony of American history: that is, that, while at least some of the spiritual descendents of the Puritans, who originally gave religious sanction to the sacred-nation concept, seem to have rejected it as being diametrically opposed to the universality of the Christian revelation and have produced critics highly sensitive to the issues of integral nationalism, the dangers of American nationalism seem to have been given little attention among Roman Catholics.

Especially may this be so today when American Catholics, viewing the struggle against Communist countries, seem so readily able to identify the cause of the nation with the cause of Christ. Actually, however, there is little evidence of an empiric nature that can be educed to indicate that nationalism is more prevalent and more intense among American Catholics than American Protestants. True, there is the contention that at least half of the members of the strongly nationalistic John Birch Society are Catholics (but, then, there are also strong nationalist Christian Front groups among fundamentalist Protestants). There are the Catholic diocesan papers (notably the Brooklyn *Tablet* and the Los Angeles *Tidings*) which consistently regard anyone who talks of internationalism as the very devil himself, and which seem to assume that the interests of this nation are the interests of God[10] (but, then, there is a great wave of nationalistic literature from a Protestant sea of political-cum-theological fundamentalism.[11] The Catholic War Veterans indeed match the hyper-patriotism of the American Legion, and there is some evidence (in the irony of the bill restricting immigration introduced by the late Senator McCarran; in the report of students in Catholic colleges hurrying to take the loyalty oath; in the widespread suspicion among Catholics of foreign aid) that, at least since the McCarthy era, the spiritual descendents of the one-hundred-percent Americans of the 1920's are likely to be lineal descendents of Catholic immigrants.[12]

So far, perhaps, this has been corroborated more by impressionistic evidence than by empirical investigation. Daniel Moynihan's quip that it is the Harvard men who are to be checked and the Fordham men who are to do the checking[13] has become a popular proverb attesting to the impression that it is among the Catholics in America today that you will find the no-nonsense Americans whose patriotism is as unswerving as their national loyalty is proven.

The reasons for the hyper-patriotism of American Catholics will, of course, be investigated later on in this book, but here it is simply noted that signs of it—not clear evidence, but the annoying, teasing evidence of smudged fingerprints—seem to be all around us. For instance, one hears that some American Protestant missionaries have relinquished their citizenship and taken on the citizenship of the country in which they have gone to reside, the reason being to show their complete identification with the people to whom they have been sent. Yet a group of Catholic missionaries in training—men who had left behind their families and who had come to see the necessity of giving up their American culture—immediately rejected the idea that they relinquish their American nationality as well, and evidently, in large measure, for reasons of an emotional, not a practical, nature.[14]

It is probably not without significance that, at the inauguration of President Johnson, January 20, 1965, while the other clergymen offered prayers which revealed America's lacks and petitioned for America's needs, the invocation of Archbishop Robert E. Lucey, of San Antonio, Texas, was in the tradition of giving testimony to the nation's superior virtues and reminding the Almighty of the nation's mission. "In Thy divine Providence, O Heavenly Father, the moral leadership of the world has been entrusted to us; the fate of humanity is in our hands; the nations look to us for survival; western civilization stands or falls with America."[15] The Rabbi's prayer, in contrast, was a chastened plea to God to give us the gift of love for all the peoples of the world, which he evidently did not take for granted—as did Archbishop Lucey.

Perhaps in the very refusal to be provoked into a discussion of the issues of nationalism and religion is to be found the best impressionistic sign of the nationalism of American Catholics. Thus, Philip Scharper, editor-in-chief of Sheed and Ward, publishers of Gordon Zahn's *German Catholics and Hitler's Wars,* reported on the few reviews of the book to appear in the Catholic press.[17] Reading over the reviews which did appear, the present writer was struck in most cases by their negative emotional tone. In the case of reviewers of evident German origin, this could be explained on the basis of their resistance to Zahn's criticism of German Catholics as *Germans.* But a more cogent explanation of the hostility of American Catholic critics (evidenced, for example, in one negative review which rather summarily dismissed the moral problem which Zahn sought to raise as simply "The perhaps inevitable consequence of the legitimate nationalism which the Church herself has never condemned."[18]) seems to be that the book itself inevitably provoked a consideration of—and a self-examination into—the issues of Catholicism and American nationalism. This reaction was rather accurately predicted

by one reviewer who wrote that the book would be maligned
and ignored, "because of the threatened triumph of . . . the
nationalistic state."[19] But it seems to the present writer that
the negative reaction can not be explained purely on such
objective grounds; in addition, there was a strong emotional
component: the book, challenging the reader's nationalism,
challenged his *identity* as an American and, as a result, was
extremely threatening.[20]

Needless to say, it is not claimed that there has been *no*
discussion of nationalism by American Catholics.[21] Mention
can be made of the pamphlet written under the auspices of
the Catholic Association for International Peace, *Patriotism,
Nationalism and the Brotherhood of Man*,[22] which distinguishes between patriotism as a virtue and what the authors
regard as the vice of nationalism. This pamphlet is notable,
however, for the way it seems to avoid actual examination of
the American Catholic historical experience. Nationalism may
be a vice, but if American Catholics have been guilty of it,
the authors are not going to stop to find out!

Mention should also be made of *National Patriotism in
Papal Teaching* by (the now Bishop) John J. Wright,[23] based
on his doctoral dissertation in theology written in the early
1940's. This book seems not only archaic in this post-Johan-
nine era of theology, but, even at the time of its publication,
it must have been open to criticism on two grounds: the author
apparently identified the evil of nationalism with "totalitarian-
ism"; he regarded any attempt to go beyond the nation-state
in ideology or organization as "dangerous liberalism." What
is especially peculiar about Wright's treatment of the relationship between religion and national patriotism is the fact that
he seems to use the latter as the way to gauge the duties of
the former; thus, he writes about the patriotic obligation
"to Catholicize the Fatherland."[24] In what seems rather a

strange reversal for a theologian whom one would expect to be anti-Durkheimian, he seems to justify religion from the point of view of what it contributes to the nation.[25] Most disappointingly, Wright's study, like the CAIP pamphlet, omits any examination of nationalism in American Catholicism.[26]

At the time of this writing, there has been no definite study of nationalism by an American Catholic which brings it under the judgment of religion in a way comparable to the studies of Marty and the two Niebuhrs. However, there is certainly increased discussion and critical examination of American national goals by American Catholics. Certainly it is evident today that the war in Vietnam and America's part in it are being subjected to moral judgment in a way that was absent in World War II when such issues as obliteration bombing caused concern only among those Catholics (and Catholic publications) who were considered by their fellows to be the lunatic fringe. Indeed, now the anniversary of Hiroshima evokes not only the fasts of Ammon Hennacy, but the sober reappraisal and expression of social responsibility by Catholics who are quite well integrated into society, but who no longer feel they can accept their nation's decisions unthinkingly. Perhaps even more indicative that Catholics are feeling increasingly responsible in facing the issues posed by nationalism (and, indeed, that they are feeling secure enough to do so) is the fact that the National Council of Catholic Men televised a dramatic adaptation of Zahn's later book.[27] This is a portrayal of the Austrian peasant who refused to serve in Hitler's army and, against the advice of ecclesiastical authority (including his own bishop) who told him it was his duty to go along with the nation, persevered in his stand and was executed for his refusal.

The same willingness to face the issue of religion and nationalism, as exemplified by the NCCM telecast, is shown in Father Bruce Vawter's *Commonweal* article, "The Beast from the Sea." He writes: "Religion is a life decision, not something infused along with American citizenship. It is a commitment of life, not a mouthful of slogans." He goes on to say that "this people and this society can achieve that to which it can legitimately aspire, to be the City of Man, only when it is capable of being measured by standards that are not of its own fashioning."[28]

Religion, if it is doing its duty to the City of Man and the Kingdom of God, can hold up these standards. It can no longer do this when it has become identified with America, when Americanism has become its own religion sufficient to itself, setting it apart from the world of man and intruding it into the world of God where sins become irremediable because the possibility of sin is removed. When religion has allowed itself to be identified with national values it has abdicated its responsibility before God. When this religion is—or was—Christianity, it has become the worship of Antichrist.[29]

The Vawter article is a criticism of the nationalism of religious people in America; it is not, however, a documentation that such nationalism actually exists, especially among American Catholics. It is our aim, therefore, to supply for the lack of published documentation and to trace the emergence of nationalism in American Catholicism.[30] To accomplish this, our investigation will focus on the life and writings of certain members of the hierarchy who seem to have had a great influence on the shaping of American Catholicism. The choice of members of the hierarchy, rather than members of the laity, can be justified by the explanation Lewy gave when he defended his use of the pronouncements of German bishops to document the relationship between the Catholic Church and Nazi Germany. He wrote: "According to Catholic teaching, of course, the Church is a corpus Christi mysticum and includes more than hierarchy and clerics. But policy and pastoral pronouncements are made by bishops, not laymen."[31]

## THE BISHOPS TO BE STUDIED

The choice of bishops, whose policy and pastoral pronouncements will be studied, is of necessity somewhat arbitrary. There can be little disagreement with the first choice, Archbishop John Carroll, first bishop to be consecrated for the United States. Of a prominent Maryland family, brother of Daniel Carroll who was a signer of the United States Constitution in 1787, and cousin of Charles Carroll of Carrollton who is memorable as one of the signers of the Declaration of Independence, John Carroll shared the interest of his relatives in the patriot cause. He participated with Benjamin Franklin in a fruitless mission to Quebec in 1776 to enlist the sympathy of the Canadians for the American Revolution. (Certain members of the Continental Congress felt that the presence of Carroll, a priest and a Jesuit, would reassure the Roman Catholic Canadians of the good intentions of the Protestant colonies.) John Carroll was more successful at the end of the war in convincing Vatican authorities that the Catholic Church in the newly-established United States should be allowed to develop, free from ecclesiastical tie-ins with either the French or the English church. Chosen by the priests assembled at Whitemarsh, Maryland, in May of 1789 as their nominee for bishop, Carroll's election was confirmed by Pope Pius VI on September 14, 1789. He became Archbishop Carroll when Baltimore was created a metropolitan see and, until his death in 1815, was influential in developing the American Church along lines that he felt were consonant with the nation's stress on freedom and civil liberties.[32]

. . . His careful delineation of the relations of the Church with Rome in spiritual matters dispelled, for those who cared to listen, any doubt about the Catholic's loyalty to his nation in political affairs. Carroll's personal patriotism and his repeated defense of his nation and her great leaders put his own loyalty above question. He was the *beau ideal* of patriot and priest to all who knew him. He defined and gave proof of the eternal compatibility of Catholic Christianity and human freedom and democratic forms.[33]

The choice of Bishop John England as the second prelate for consideration here may not be so obvious as the choice of Archbishop Carroll. Yet, from the time he arrived in the United States in 1820, John England (who was born in Ireland in 1786) had an influence that went far beyond the borders of his own impoverished diocese of Charleston and its few thousand Catholics.[34] Until his death in 1842, Bishop England was certainly the most vocal, if not, indeed, the most influential, Catholic bishop in the United States. Through his speaking engagements throughout the country, and particularly through his writings in the *United States Catholic Miscellany* which he established in 1822, Bishop England's thoughts on the problems and on the future of the Catholic Church in the United States, on the relationship of Catholics with their fellow Americans, and in defense of Catholicism from the charges of her critics, were presented to American Catholics and non-Catholics as well. Evidently from the time of his arrival in the United States, the Charleston ordinary was aware of the need for the Catholic bishops to assemble together and plan and legislate for the American Church as a whole. Unable to move Archbishop Maréchal of Baltimore to convoke a provincial council (synod), Bishop England was more successful with Maréchal's successor.

The first provincial council of Baltimore in 1829 was dominated by the thinking of Bishop England, and he continued to play a leading role in the deliberations and in writing the documents of succeeding councils in 1833, 1837 and 1840. However, he was not interested in seeing that only bishops got together for democratic deliberations; in his own diocese, according to the terms of the Constitution he wrote, there were to be yearly conventions attended by members of a House of the Clergy and a House of Lay Delegates. He viewed this, his personal solution to the problem of trusteeism, as an especially fitting way of bringing the Church into harmony with American values. According to Guilday, Bishop England "was an American with all that mystical love for America which is visible in the leaders of the earlier days of the nation's history," who had a "thorough grasp of American idealism" and "made for himself a unique place in American history."[35]

Like Bishop England, John Hughes—Bishop, then Archbishop, of New York from January 7, 1838 until his death, January 3, 1864—was born in Ireland. However, unlike England who emigrated upon his appointment as an American bishop, Hughes came to the United States in 1817 at the age of twenty and studied for the priesthood in this country. Ordained in 1826 as a priest of the Philadelphia diocese, Father Hughes distinguished himself in a short time by his success in debating Protestant clergymen on religious topics. Even after he had become ordinary of New York, his extensive public lecturing continued. His occupation of the New York See at the time when the city was playing an increasingly prominent part in the economic, social, intellectual and political life of the nation meant that John Hughes was in the obvious position to speak for the Catholic Church of the United States. Asked by Secretary of State Seward to plead the Union cause in France, the New York prelate was proud to perform this mission on behalf of his country. In his writings and speeches up until the time of his death, Archbishop

Hughes was concerned to defend the loyalty of his Catholic people, a large proportion of whom had come to New York in the great wave of migration from Ireland during the 1840's. Typical of his thought and style are the following sentences:

> I understand the rights of a citizen, and the duties also. I understand the genius, and constitution, and history of the country. My feelings, and habits, and thoughts, have been so much identified with all that is American; that I had almost forgotten I was a foreigner, until recent circumstances have brought it too painfully to my recollection . . . I can even now remember my reflections, on first beholding the American flag. It never crossed my mind that a time might come, when that flag, the emblem of the freedom just alluded to, should be divided, by apportioning its *stars* to the citizens of native birth, and its *stripes* only, as the portion of the foreigner.[36]

Another Irish-born American bishop who was to play a prominent part in explaining Catholicism to an American public was John Ireland, made coadjutor bishop of St. Paul, Minnesota, in 1875, and archbishop in 1888. Archbishop Ireland has been summed up as "a man of progressive outlook, a sane liberal, a statesman, a non-professional educator, a humanitarian, a civic leader, and, above all, a churchman with something of the ruling medieval ecclesiastical about his heroic character."[37] A military chaplain during the Civil War, he was destined to play an important part in various secular diplomatic negotiations both before and after the Spanish-American War. Until his death in 1918, Archbishop Ireland figured profoundly in every significant controversy among American Catholics. Unlike the prelates mentioned thus far in this chapter, Archbishop Ireland not only interpreted Catholicism to Americans, but he also interpreted America, and especially the American Church, to the Catholics of Europe. Deeply involved in the controversy over Americanism (and the so-called Americanist heresy),[38] impatient with those Catholics, priests and people, who desired to keep the language and traditions of the country from which they emigrated, Archbishop Ireland opted for rapid Americanization. An ardent defender of the American system of separation of Church and State, he evidently missed the irony in the fact that he asked his friend Theodore Roosevelt, as President of the United States, to petition the Vatican that he be created a cardinal. As pugnacious as Roosevelt, Ireland showed himself equally as vehement in his nationalism. Through Dennis O'Connell, a mutual friend and agent at the Vatican, Archbishop Ireland became connected with Senator Albert Beveridge of Indiana. Evidence that he was as flamboyant and as outspoken in his nationalism as Senator Beveridge can be found in the addresses collected in the volume, *The Church and Modern Society*.[39]

Of more temperate speech than Archbishop Ireland and marked by a much more quiet demeanor was the American Cardinal, James Gibbons. His long life as a member of the hierarchy spanned the years from 1868, when he was appointed to the Vicariate of North Carolina, until 1921, when he died after occupying the see of Baltimore for almost forty-four years.

Born in Baltimore in 1834, Gibbons was taken to Ireland by his Irish-born parents when he was three years old, not to return to the United States until 1853. From that time on, Gibbons' life was immersed in the life of the developing American Church. According to his biographer Ellis, Cardinal Gibbons was friendly with every American president from Cleveland on. Usually on the liberal side with his friend Archbishop Ireland in most controversies, he saved the Knights of Labor from condemnation by Rome. His *Faith of Our Fathers* became a classic explanation of Catholicism to American

Protestants, and his long life was spent in interpreting the Church to America and America to the Church.[40]

To bring the case study of American Catholicism up to the present, the choice of Francis Cardinal Spellman for consideration seems a fairly obvious one. Archbishop of New York since 1939 and a close friend of Pope Pius XII, certainly through the latter's pontificate (and probably up until the time of the actual assembling of the Second Vatican Council) he was considered to be the spokesman for the American Church. The prelate, to whom the press turned for the authoritative statements on the American Catholic viewpoint, was known to be Franklin D. Roosevelt's favorite bishop. For a while there was popular speculation that Cardinal Spellman would become the first American pope. His break with Roosevelt over the President's policy toward Russia seems, if anything, to have intensified his expressions of ardent patriotism. His trips to visit American Armed Forces during and since World War II have been a logical fulfillment of his role as ordinary for the military services. Whether or not Cardinal Spellman has gone beyond the requirements of this role, whether or not his expressions of patriotism have veered in the direction of uncritical and intense nationalism—these questions may be investigated by anyone taking the trouble to read his published books. His official biography does not seem to contradict the self-portrait given in his own writings.[41]

Archbishop Carroll, Bishop England, Archbishops Hughes and Ireland, Cardinals Gibbons and Spellman—these, then, are the members of the American hierarchy whose lives and pronouncements will be investigated for evidence of nationalism. For a "control," it has been decided to use Bishop John Lancaster Spalding.[42] A liberal who was extremely influential in the foundation of The Catholic University of America, Bishop Spalding, Peoria's first ordinary, seems to have provided an intellectual leaven in American Catholicism until his death in 1916.[43] Seemingly forgotten today (a full-length biography of John Lancaster Spalding has only recently been published),[44] and certainly in his day not so influential as his contemporaries Cardinal Gibbons and Archbishop Ireland, he was, nevertheless, a prolific writer and lecturer. Merle Curti singles out Bishop Spalding as a leading Catholic thinker who "deplored the tendency to regard the nation as the supreme end of life . . . No voice in the Roman Church was more eloquent, more closely akin to the temper of the Emersonian insistence on the higher law of truth and morality than that of Bishop Spalding of Peoria."[45] Because he evidently saw the dangers of hyper-patriotism and the uncritical acceptance of the nationalistic spirit, Bishop Spalding makes an interesting foil for the other prelates who have been selected for this study. Analyses of his writings will be left for a future chapter; suffice it to note here that Peoria's ordinary, from an old American family, evidently did not suffer the same psychological need to prove his Americanism. Nephew of Martin John Spalding, one-time Archbishop of Baltimore, he probably sensed no great burden to prove the compatibility of Catholicism and American citizenship.[46]

More defensive about their Americanism were Bishop England, Archbishop Ireland and Archbishop Hughes who were born in Ireland, and Cardinal Gibbons who spent his formative years there.

## IRISH NATIONALISM IN THE BACKGROUND

When a Jesuit historian, in the course of reading a paper at a meeting of the American Catholic Historical Association in 1927, asked, "Is America to be *Irland it Mikla,* a Greater Ireland?",[47] he posed a question which Irish immigrants to the United States had been answering in the affirmative for at least the past hundred years. Identifying America with

Ireland as a Land of Destiny, young Irishmen like Michael Forrest, who arrived at the age of seventeen in the United States, could express regret at being born too late to fight in the war against the British "to save a nation from base tyranny, and gain freedom for posterity."[48] Another young Irishman, Matthew Carey, driven from Ireland at the age of twenty-four because he called for armed insurrection against England, made the *Pennsylvania Herald* the mouthpiece for violent opposition to the British.[49] Unlike Forrest and Carey, certainly some at least of the Irish did come in time to fight the English in the Revolution. Guilday commented on the influence of the Irish schoolmasters who, having escaped from Ireland, taught in private homes and schools in the American colonies, and he asked (somewhat extravagantly): "Who shall say it was not through them principally that the colonies began the work of severance across the Atlantic?"[50]

The point here is not, of course, Guilday's historical accuracy. In the tie-in of American nationalism with Irish nationalism, what mattered more than whether the Irish immigrants actually fanned the flame of the American Revolution was that in spirit (in retrospect) they thought they did. Ireland's enemy and America's enemy were the same,[51] and the Irish immigrant to America had apparently no trouble in identifying the loyalty he bore America with the loyalty he bore his native land. As John Talbot Smith remarked of the Irish Catholic immigrants to New York "who brought with them from their native country a great knowledge of the Republic, profound admiration for its success over England, and true affection for its principles":

. . . These people became more American than the Americans, and knew how to appreciate the blessings of civic freedom far better than the natives, who had always enjoyed such blessings. They looked up to the Fathers of the Republic as to the saints,[52] kept the national holidays with a fervor that surprised all, and took the oath of allegiance to the United States with a fervor the deeper that they were asked to foreswear allegiance to King George . . .[53]

In like vein, and in specific mention of Bishop England, another chronicler of the Irish in America, wrote:

. . . Like all Irishmen, of that day as of the present, Bishop England at once became an American citizen, thoroughly identified with his adopted country, proud of her greatness, jealous of her honour, loving her beyond all others, save that old land whose recollection lay warm in his heart.[54]

Indeed, while delivering the annual address on St. Patrick's Day, 1824, to the Hibernian Society in Savannah, Georgia, Bishop England is said to have appeared in the pulpit, "with a cross formed with shamrocks on his stole"[55]—fitting symbol not only of the Irish patriotism which, for him and other Irish immigrants, had become one with their American loyalty, but also of the perhaps more crucial "fusion of religion and nationalism in the Irish mind."[56]

In the long centuries of struggle against a foreign and a Protestant master, the Irish had identified their struggle for their faith with their struggle for the preservation of themselves as a nation. Their religion and their nationalism were one. Daniel O'Connell's cause of Emancipation would have failed, it is said, were it not for the Irish priests who stood at the church doors and encouraged their people in his support.[57] The sentiment behind their actions is explained by a biographer of Bishop England who, explaining how England threw himself, heart and soul, into the work of Emancipation in the years after 1812, wrote: "At the period of which we write, the Irish priesthood had been traitors to their religion, had they been faithless to their country. The party dominant in the land proclaimed 'war to the knife' against Catholicism, and political disabilities were but another name for religious oppression."[58] When the *Cork Mercentile Chronicle*, organ of the liberal party, began to fail, John England revived the journal and became its editor. Fighting for Emancipation and agitating against Vetoism, which would have permitted the British government to exercise a veto over candidates for the Irish bishoprics, the new editor is said to have conducted the *Chronicle* according to "sentiments of genuine patriotism, regulated by Christian morality."[59]

It is interesting to note, parenthetically, that for England and his biographers—as, later, for Hughes—the French Revolution was evil; the American Revolution which could be identified with the continuing Irish revolt was Christian and good. Hughes went a step further and disapproved revolutions in principle: "The Church does not recognize the principle that the people may change their government when they will." But, according to Hughes, the "American Revolutionists were different because they were aware of God's Providence."[60]

Archbishop Hughes, in extolling the merits of Daniel O'Connell, remarked on one occasion that "O'Connell had but two predominant ideas—loves: the one was the love of his country, the other of his creed,—and in his public life, two became one and indivisible."[61] With this description of O'Connell, Hughes could indeed have been describing himself, Bishop England, or many another Catholic priest or prelate, Irish or Irish-American, among his predecessors or successors.[62] In his native land, to be a true Irishman was to be a Catholic, and to be a Catholic was to be a true Irishman —an equation which the immigrant imported with him to America. As Herberg writes:

. . . His Americanism took on the same religious fervor and soon came to be identified with his Catholicism. It was almost as if to be a Catholic meant somehow to be an American, even though it was obvious that the converse was not as true as it had been in Ireland . . . Irish, Catholic, and American became almost identical in the Irish-American mind, and the Americanism of the Irish Catholic developed into something much more than merely the sense of national 'belonging.' To a greater or lesser degree all American Catholicism has tended to take on this peculiar nationalistic coloration.[63]

If, then, for the Irish-American—as for the Irishman— nationalism and religion were thus intertwined,[64] and his identity as a Catholic and as an American posed no problem and no intrinsic contradiction for him, why has he been so defensive through the years about his Americanism? Why— as documentation in the following chapters will indicate—did the prelates we are studying find it necessary to speak out again and again on the dual theme: *how Catholic America is* and *how American the Catholic Church is?* Granted, the Irishman came to America with a certain pugnacity about his religion and his nationalism, an attitude developed in the years of struggle under the domination of alien Protestants. But this pugnacity was fostered, and the need to demonstrate his loyalty as a Catholic American (which might otherwise have lain dormant) was brought to the surface by the difficulties he encountered as an immigrant. His nationalism cannot be explained without taking account of the various nativist movements.[65]

## NATIVISM PROVOKING NATIONALISM

In his *Relation* to Propaganda, dated April 23, 1792, Carroll petitioned the Holy See that the Missal and Breviary supplements for England be dropped from use in America. His explanation was that "the Irish clergy in the United States refused to celebrate the English saints."[66] In so writing, Carroll was indicating that a change had already taken place in the composition of the clergy in the infant Church of America. The approximately thirty priests who were present in the colonies at the time of the Revolution[67] were, for the most part, former members of the English province of the recently-dissolved Society of Jesus. The faithful to whom they ministered, especially in Maryland, tended to be well-established families (like the Carrolls themselves) differing from their neighbors, not in culture or class, but in religion alone.

Within a brief span of years, however, conditions were to change: the priests were increasingly to have been born in Ireland, ministering to people of similar ethnic origin. As has been indicated, these Irish immigrants tended to possess a strong Irish nationalism which they were ready to transmute into American nationalism.[68] Bishop England at once reveals the hurt and chagrin of the Irishman wanting to identify completely as an American; at the same time, he gives the *rationale* behind the rejection he and his fellow Irish Catholics encountered, when he writes (in a letter to the Society for the Propagation of the Faith at Lyons, explaining the difficulties regarding the progress of the Catholic religion in the United States):

. . . the vast majority of the Catholic population of the United States are descendants of those men, of whose struggles at home for the preservation of their religion and the defence of their country, I have endeavoured to trace an outline. England has, unfortunately, too well succeeded in linking contumely to their name in all her colonies; and though the United States may have cast away the yoke under which she held them, many other causes combined to continue against the Irish Catholic, more or less, to the present day. . . . That which more than a century of fashion has made habitual, is not to be overcome in a year, and to any Irish Catholic who has dwelt in this country during one-fourth of the period of my sojourn, it will be painfully plain that, although the evil is slowly diminishing, its influence is not confined to the American nor to the anti-Catholic. When a race is once degraded, however unjustly, it is a weakness of our nature that, however we may be identified with them upon some points, we are desirous of showing that the similitude is not complete. You may be an Irishman but not a Catholic; you may be Catholic but not Irish; it is clear you are not an Irish Catholic in either case! But when the great majority of the Catholics in the United States were either Irish or of Irish descent, the force of the prejudice against the Irish Catholic bore against the Catholic religion in the United States: and the influence of this prejudice has been far more mysterious than is generally believed.[69]

Bishop England was writing about five years after a mob had burned the Ursuline Convent in Charlestown, Massachusetts, in August of 1834, perhaps the most notorious example of the results of anti-Catholic mob action. It was, however, in no sense unique: St. Mary's Church in New York City had been set afire in 1831, and attacks on Catholic churches in New England had become so frequent that insurance companies refused to place a policy upon Catholic buildings which were not constructed of noninflammable materials.[70] Billington, in his account of nativism from the years 1800 to 1860, evidently regards the burning of the convent in Charlestown as an especially virulent example of anti-Catholicism. He notes that, while the existence of a plan to burn the convent was known at least three days before the actual burning, no move was made against the rioters because public opinion gave tacit approval to the project.[71] Editors and ministers throughout the nation, while willing to deplore the actual violence, took the occasion of the Charlestown burning to add that "the Ursuline convent and all convents should be done away with to prevent the conversion of Protestant girls to Catholicism, and the spread of immorality throughout the United States."[72]

In a trial which parallels the contemporary trials of the slayers of civil-rights workers, eight men were acquitted of the capital offense of arson, but not before the anti-Catholic nature of the proceedings had been clearly demonstrated and the Mother Superior of the convent, as well as Bishop Fenwick, cross-examined on the immorality of convent life.[73]

So-called "disclosures" of the evils of the Catholic convents remained a focal point for rallying anti-Catholic nativist senti-ment. From the time of its publication in 1836 until the start of the Civil War, the *Awful Disclosures* of Maria Monk sold some 300,000 copies and continued to inflame the nativist sentiments which had originally caused it to be written.[74] By the mid-1840's, according to Billington, the Protestant churches were able to present a united front against Catholi-cism;[75] the nativism of the 1830's, which was a lower-class phenomenon, had been replaced by a middle-class Protestant nativism which came about as a reaction to the school question and the report of Catholic attempts to burn the Bible.[76] In the 1840's and 1850's there were at least five hundred Catholic casualties. What amounted to a popular hysteria was gripping many sections of the country; a rumor that Irish servant girls were being instructed to poison the food of their Protestant employers swept through New England in 1855,[77] receiving as much credence as the report in the mid-thirties that the Pope coveted the Mississippi valley and was sending Catholic immigrants westward to take control.[78]

In 1837, and again in 1840, the Catholic bishops of the United States assembled in council and issued letters express-ing their sorrow at the anti-Catholic actions and sentiments of some of their fellow Americans.[79] Certainly it seems true that nativism (which Higham defines as "intense opposition to an internal minority on the ground of its foreign, i.e., 'un-Ameri-can,' connections," through which "runs the connecting, ener-

gizing force of modern nationalism"[80]) in the years before the
Civil War was synonymous with anti-Catholicism.

Demonstrated throughout the 1840's and 1850's were
"the traditional ideological ingredients (of the religious xeno-
phobia): ex-priests lecturing on the moral iniquities of con-
fessional and convent; warnings about Catholic political
conspiracies; widespread rumors that the faithful were drilling
nightly in church basements in preparation for an armed
uprising."[81] It is not surprising that Catholics, finding themselves so attacked, should react defensively, proclaiming their
Americanism and reaffirming their national loyalty in increasingly extravagant terms. If Protestants regarded Catholics as
yoked to a foreign religious despotism, Catholics were evidently moved to react in a way which combined apologetic
defense of the Faith with re-affirmation of national patriotism.
The Breckinridge-Hughes debates in 1835, for instance, attracted widespread comment and a goodly readership when
they were later published.[82] After he had become the ordinary
of New York, John Hughes continued his verbal defense of
Catholicism in lecture and published writing, but at least on
one occasion the activities of the nativists provoked him to
take more aggressive measures. According to his biographer:

Hughes openly blamed the Catholics of Philadelphia for not defending their churches during nativist riots . . . He was ready for
a desperate struggle if the mob forced one upon him. He caused
each church in the city [New York] to be occupied by an armed
force of one or two thousand men "resolved, after taking as many
lives as they could in defense of their property, to give up, if
necessary, their own lives for the same cause."[83]

Kohn, for one, blames Archbishop Hughes for the fears
which, in the first place, inspired some of the nativist activities.
He writes that these fears were fanned

by the uncompromising attitude then adopted by the Catholic
church. Its spiritual leader in America, Archbishop John Hughes
of New York, proclaimed in 1850 that "the object we hope to
accomplish in time, is to convert all Pagan nations, and all
Protestant nations, even England with her proud parliament and
imperial sovereign. It is a commission of God to his church and
not a human project."[84]

Certainly this project of conversion was interpreted by the
nativists as including more than spiritual dominance. Spurred
on by such writers as Samuel F. B. Morse, artist and inventor,
who set out to prove that the Austrian mission society—the
Leopoldine Association—was pouring gold into the United
States to undermine the national Protestant faith as well as
American political institutions,[85] the nativist movement of the
1840's evolved into the Know-Nothing party of the '50's which
did succeed in capturing some very important political offices.
Billington notes that "although both the order and the party
into which it grew professed vehement enmity for immigrants,
the motive behind the whole Know-Nothing movement was
hatred of Catholicism." Indeed, Protestant aliens who were
zealous against Popery were openly welcomed into the party.
"The Know-Nothing party was really a No-Popery party,
despite all the gloss and fine phrases in its pronouncements."[86]
In the elections of 1854 the Know-Nothing party achieved
major victories, with about 75 Congressmen being sent to
Washington on the pledge that they would carry the nation
into a war against the Pope and his followers. The party swept
victoriously through Massachusetts: the governor and all state
officers were Know-Nothings; the state Senate was made up
entirely of members of this party, and the state House of
Representatives was composed of one Whig, one Free Soiler
and 376 Know-Nothings. The following year saw the triumph
of the Know-Nothing party in other New England states, as

well as in Maryland, Kentucky, New York, Pennsylvania, and California. In fact, so great was the vote which the Know-Nothings achieved in most of the southern states and throughout the country (with the exception of the northwest) that not only did party members expect to place their candidate in the White House in 1856, but even such Catholic papers as the Boston *Pilot* accepted the inevitability of a Know-Nothing president.[87]

It is a continuing irony that the Irish Catholics, who were most eager for assimilation and are credited for successfully integrating Catholics as a whole into the American nation,[88] should, through the nineteenth century, continue to attract the particular hostility of the nativists.[89] However, that this should have been so in the "nationalist nineties" is rather more understandable than it was early in the century. The reaction to the Democratic victories of 1890 and 1892 which worked to the advantage of Irish politicians was one of increased anti-Catholic feeling, and the American Protective Association (A.P.A.) "effectively exploited both the political ambitions and the broad national anxieties on which anti-Catholicism throve."[90] Not realizing that certainly the sources of immigration had changed over the years, the A.P.A. continued to rail against an Irish influx. The movement soon lost steam, but not before Archbishop Ireland took the wind out of its sails by an address in which he himself publicly adopted the A.P.A. principles.[91]

Cardinal Gibbons did not so blatantly follow Archbishop Ireland's evident psychology of "if you can't lick them, join them." Like Archbishop Ireland, however, he did respond to the threat of nativism and took advantage of every opportunity to proclaim the loyalty of American Catholics. "It is a sacred duty for every American to do all in his power to perpetuate our civil institutions and to avert the dangers which threaten them."[92]

## NATIONALITIES AND NATIONALISM

It is not surprising that Archbishop Ireland and Cardinal Gibbons, given the renewed manifestations of nativism during the 1890's, should have become particularly annoyed with their German Catholic brethren in America who, they believed, unfeelingly provided fuel for the flame. The controversy between the Catholic liberals, who opted for rapid Americanization of the immigrants,[93] and those bishops and priests mainly of German origin who believed preservation of the immigrant's language and his faith were linked—a controversy which had, to a degree, lain dormant before the 1880's —erupted violently and for the entire American public to see when the famous Lucerne Memorial was forwarded to the Vatican in April, 1891. Under the aegis of Peter Cahensly, a German layman who had dedicated most of his life to the spiritual care of German emigrants, a congress of prominent Catholics from several European countries met at Lucerne. It petitioned the Holy See, among other things, that more foreign-speaking prelates be installed in America. As could be expected, Cardinal Gibbons and Archbishop Ireland reacted with great alarm, the latter, especially, taking steps to put down the threat.

Cross comments:

. . . The liberals' offensive against the Germans stemmed in part from nothing more exalted than the desire to eliminate the only significant resistance to the Irish-American domination of the hierarchy; but in an era when pan-Germanism was alarming a good deal of the world, the persistence of a group of the faithful in proclaiming that their Catholicism and their Germanism were closely linked gave the liberals a more exalted justification for their crusade.[94]

Of course, the intra-mural struggle for control of the Catholic Church in America, to which Cross refers, had been going on for the past century. And as early as 1788, John Carroll was arbitrating the difficulties which had arisen in Philadelphia between Germans and Irish[95] and, shortly thereafter, between the French and the Irish (both clergy and people) in Boston.[96] As early as 1798 a petition was made to Propaganda that the Germans of the United States be given a German bishop for themselves.[97] Bishop England's *Life* contains numerous references to his quarrels with Archbishop Maréchal and other French bishops in America as well as to his pleas that more truly "American" (in Bishop England's context, read "Irish") bishops be appointed.[98]

To interpret the nationalities' controversy as a simple conflict of interest (a maneuvering for power) would be grossly incorrect, however. Certainly by the time of Cardinal Gibbons and Archbishop Ireland (and, indeed, even in Bishop England's day) there was a strong value element involved. Resistance to Cahenslyism, Gibbons and Ireland felt, was necessary not just to insure that the Germans would not rule the Church in America, but "to make it possible that a Catholic Church could exist in America at all."[99] Both prelates, Ireland and Gibbons, wanted the Irish Catholic Benevolent Union to drop the word "Irish" from its title[100] because they felt that foreign nationalism—of whatever kind—was dangerous to the interests of Catholicism in the United States. Their desire to see the Catholic immigrant pursue rapid Americanization was met with the wish of many of the German clergy that their people keep the German language and culture in order to keep the faith. If the first position was expressed by Archbishop Ireland in his declaration that no immigrant who was unwilling to be assimilated immediately deserved admission to this country,[101] then the second was expressed by Father Anton H.

Walburg, pastor of St. Augustine's Church, Cincinnati: "De-
nationalization is demoralization. It degrades and debases
human nature. A foreigner who loses his nationality is in
danger of losing his faith and character."[102]

Even more extreme statements of the stand against Americanization had been made by Nicholas Gonner, editor of the
*Katholischer Westen.* Gonner not only advised parents to respond with the rod to every attempt of their children to speak
English, but he also advocated that German bishops should
go to Germany to obtain their priests and that they should
send young men of German extraction to seminaries in Germany to prepare for ordination. It was Gonner who had stated
that German Catholics in America should not consider themselves beholden as guests of the Anglo-Americans, since Catholic Germany, under Charles V, owned the land of America
before any Anglo-American did.[103]

If Gonner's writing was atypical of the German position
in being more extreme, it was typical in urging a continued
German-Catholic separation. The activities of the Central
Verein, the separate German priests' society, and the annual
assembly of German Catholics in a Katholikentag evoked the
misgivings of the members of the American hierarchy. Made
anxious by the nativists and eager themselves to have Catholics
undergo rapid Americanization, the American hierarchy saw
in them evidence of unhealthy foreignism. Archbishop Ireland,
in refusing to bless a projected Minnesota Katholikentag,
wrote on August 6, 1888, that certain parts of its program
were indicative of what he called "a spirit of ultra-nationalism,
hardly consistent with the fullness of Catholic unity which
should characterize the life of the Church in America."[104]

The Cahensly episode, which, to Archbishop Ireland, represented German nationalism in its most blatant form, also
presented to him and other Americanizers among the Ameri-

can bishops an opportunity for a definitive triumph. Denouncing to the press the impudence of foreigners in attempting to interfere in American Catholic affairs, Archbishop Ireland evidently used all avenues he could think of not only to insure that the Holy See would turn down Cahensly's proposals, but also to assure himself that the Catholics of America would emerge as triumphantly patriotic in the eyes of their fellow Americans. Thus, on the basis of press reports from the Vatican sent out by his friend Dennis O'Connell—reports which insinuated that Cahenslyism was a plot of the Prussian government—Archbishop Ireland convinced American journalists of German political aggression, and he persuaded Senator Cushman Davis to attack it on the floor of the United States Senate.[105]

After the Vatican had given a negative response to the Lucerne Memorial, not only was the nationalities' issue in the American Church settled conclusively, but the essential patriotism of American Catholics was also successfully vindicated. Both Cardinal Gibbons and Archbishop Ireland had special reason to rejoice at the successful resolution of the crisis when President Benjamin Harrison expressed himself to the Cardinal as being very pleased with his strong condemnation of the Cahensly movement.[106]

But the resolution might not have been so simple and decisive as those prelates thought. Was the issue of specific nationalities in the Church (and their accompanying nationalisms) resolved only to leave unquestioned, unprobed, the issue of the relationship of the Catholic Church in America to the rising spirit of nationalism? True, as Barry notes, the German leaders, in their insistence on the preservation of specific German Catholicism, were lacking in contact with the strong spirit of nationalism that was sweeping the country;[107] but were prelates like Gibbons and Ireland so much in contact with it

—indeed so attuned to it—that they could not recognize that American nationalism, too, could pose a dilemma for the Church? If Archbishop Ireland could note that "a spirit of ultra-nationalism" was "hardly consistent with the fullness of Catholic *unity*,"[108] should he have been expected to note that it was also inconsistent with Catholic *universality*?[109]

Indeed, did the need of Archbishop Ireland, Cardinal Gibbons and those Catholic prelates who went before them to identify themselves and their people with the American nation cause them to be heedless of the prophetic function of religion as judge of the nation? Given the background of Irish nationalism, of the nativist movements, and of the nationalities controversy in the Catholic Church in America, this, understandably, could happen. Whether it *did* happen is a question which will next be considered in the documentation of the words and actions of the prelates chosen for this study of nationalism in American Catholicism.

## NOTES

[1] So speaks Craddock, after forty years as an American Protestant missionary in China, in Richard McKenna's *The Sand Pebbles* (Greenwich, Conn.: Crest Books, 1964), p. 494.

[2] Merle Curti, *The Roots of American Loyalty*, gives extensive documentation of the criticism of American chauvinism, especially in the period after the Civil War and after World War I.

[3] Curti, *ibid.*, p. 239, points out that after World War I the criticism of one-hundred-percent patriotism sprang not only "from the humane and liberal American tradition of faith in testing general concepts by facts and results and focusing on them the light of reason. It also rested in the equally traditional Christian conception of a higher law than that of man. The vigorous and broad-based contribution of the churches to the peace movement in the post-war decade, accompanied as it was by a criticism of one-hundred-percent Americanism, issued in the last

analysis from the faith that when the altar and the flag are in conflict, the altar takes precedence. It would, in fact, be hard to overemphasize this element in the criticisms of the chauvinistic patriotism of the postwar years."

⁴ See, for instance, H. Richard Niebuhr, "Christ Against Culture," in Louis Schneider, *Religion, Culture and Society* (New York: Wiley, 1964). Reinhold Niebuhr, particularly in *The Irony of American History*, also shows his concern for the future of an America which pretends to a national purity, sanctioned by religion, which he feels is beyond the capacity of any nation. In this connection see also, Niebuhr and Heimert, *A Nation So Conceived*, pp. 126–128: "A sense of mission may be a source of confusion when it tempts nations with a messianic consciousness to hide the inevitable vital impulses of collective existence, chiefly the will to power, under the veil of its ideal purposes. Such nations are inclined to pretend that they have triumphed over the baser impulses and to be wholly devoted to ideal ends. In the American case the temptation is compounded by the obvious success of a nation which has grown so rapidly in strength by grace of various geographic, economic, and historic factors. The inclination is to attribute the growth in power to our democratic virtues. The pretension of superior virtue of a particularly powerful nation is bound to prove vexatious to even the friendliest and closest allies . . . Our national history, particularly the history of our relation to other nations in the world community of nations, is bound to exhibit not only the virtues of a commitment but also various compounds of the two temptations to which messianic nations are prone: The temptation to pretend a purity of motive which is beyond the capacity of nations, and may be beyond the capacity of individuals, and the temptation to rely on a prematurely fixed content and substance of our messianic destiny. In our case that would be the preservation and extension of democratic self government."

⁵ Martin E. Marty, *Varieties of Unbelief* (New York: Holt, Rinehart and Winston, 1964), p. 171.

⁶ *Ibid.*, pp. 162–163.

⁷ *Ibid.*, p. 165.

⁸ *Ibid.*, p. 171.

⁹ *Ibid.*, p. 170. Yet this very fact of the acceptability of nationalism as a parallel religion for adherents of historic faiths gets them into

some disagreement with their fellow nationalists. Thus Marty notes that: "The Supreme Court decisions which rule out imposed prayers in public schools produced double reactions among nationalists. Some who were determinedly secularist would like to see an integral religion of democracy become formally established, and they regard the removal of historic forms of devotion as a step in this direction. Others who interpret culture sacrally want to see religious and specifically Christian elements reintroduced in the culture, partly in order to continue justifying the Christianity-and-nationalism tie . . ." *Loc. cit.*

[10] Among Catholic liberals there has been great glee in watching to see how such papers manage to handle, hide—or bury—such documents as *Mater et Magistra* and *Pacem in Terris*, the very antithesis of the nationalistic spirit with their calls for international organization and cooperation.

[11] While the fundamentalist periodicals seem to be more overt in their nationalism, as Marty notes (*op. cit.*, p. 171), the mingling of Christianity with nationalism can be found among "fundamentalist and modernist alike." Among the latter, the expression of nationalism is, at the same time, probably more subtle and more sophisticated.

In his *The Emergence of Liberal Catholicism in America* (Cambridge, Mass.: Harvard University Press, 1958), p. 44, Robert Cross notes that "the conservative McQuaid was as nationalistic as . . . Ireland"—a salutary reminder to us that, while the American nationalism of the last century is associated more prominently with liberal Catholic prelates, liberalism has no monopoly on it.

In the historical reversal, it is apparent that today nationalism is not exclusively the prerogative of conservative Catholics. For instance, participating in a Mass with an avant-garde group of liturgical liberals, the writer noted that, at the memento for the dead, remembrance was made for "*Our* soldiers who died in Vietnam" with the same unconscious nationalism found in the most conservative parish.

[12] See E. Digby Baltzell, *The Protestant Establishment* (New York: Random House, 1964), and Nathan Glazer and Daniel Patrick Moynihan, *Beyond the Melting Pot* (Cambridge, Mass.: MIT Press, 1963), particularly "The Irish," pp. 217–287.

[13] *Ibid.*, p. 271.

[14] The writer is indebted to Mr. W. W. Parkinson of the Division of Overseas Ministries, National Council of the Churches of Christ, for

the information that this practice of taking out citizenship in the mission country (notably in Brazil) has gone on for the past decade, and to Joseph P. Fitzpatrick, S.J., for the example of the reaction of the Catholic missionaries in training at the Center for Inter-Cultural Formation, Cuernavaca, Mexico.

The issue of citizenship is a complicated one for missionaries and it has been given widespread discussion by missionaries of many nations. But Father Fitzpatrick reports his distinct impression that, when the question is simply raised with citizens of many nations, the response of Americans (United States) has an emotional charge to it that is not evident in the citizens of other nations.

The writer would also like to mention the reaction of a group of priests, whom she taught, to Herberg's book, *Protestant-Catholic-Jew*. The fact that they were unable to see any validity to his thesis, and particularly their inability to see the possibility of any conflict between Christian values and national goals—they finally hit on an example of such a possibility in the case of an American Catholic soldier asked to bomb the Vatican—seemed to provide evidence to corroborate the thesis itself.

[15] The complete text of Archbishop Lucey's Invocation follows:

Almighty and eternal God, we ask a blessing upon all who are gathered here today to honor the Chief Executive of our nation and our Vice President. We thank Thee for peace and prosperity; we are grateful for fertile soil, abundant harvests and the fruits of the earth by which we live. But we remember that man does not live by bread alone and we are grateful, too, for *the spiritual heritage of our nation—a sense of justice to all mankind, a spirit of charity to the lowly and the oppressed.* (Italics mine.)

In Thy divine Providence, O Heavenly Father, the moral leadership of the world has been entrusted to us; the fate of humanity is in our hands; the nations look to us for survival; western civilization stands or falls with America. In these days of tragedy and crisis all that we hold dear is challenged; belief in God, respect for human personality, honor, integrity, the very freedom of the human spirit—all these are at stake and our country, a champion of truth and justice, must lead the nations of the world to the dawn of a brighter hope.

We pray that Almighty God may grant to the leader of our country wisdom and understanding, strength and courage. In these days of stress and strife, in the hour of fateful decision, may God make clear to our President the path of honor and of peace, the path of freedom and justice, the path of brotherhood and truth—that truth that makes men free. Amen.

[16] The writer is aware that an alternate explanation can be offered

for the differences in the two prayers. The prayer offered by the Archbishop seems to be marked by the *triumphalism* lamented by Bishop
De Smedt and other bishops at the Vatican council. However, this
spiritual complacency—the smug assurance of belonging to a Church
whose stand is always righteous—is easily united with the nationalism
that precludes the nation's ever being in the wrong.

[17] Private communication to the present writer.

[18] Robert Graham, S.J., *America*, April 28, 1962.

[19] Herbert C. Burke, *Perspectives*, May-June, 1962.

[20] The present writer does not mean to imply that Zahn's book was
above criticism. However, the precise point is this: the book's methodo-
logical and sociological deficiencies were ignored, and Catholic reviewers tended to react emotionally.

[21] See the perceptive article by John La Farge, S.J., "Three Main
Causes of Nationalism," *Thought*, IX, 2, Sept., 1934, pp. 181–192.

[22] New York: Paulist Press, 1937.

[23] Westminster, Md.: Newman, 1943.

[24] Wright, *op. cit.*, p. 93.

[25] It is hard to tell, without going over the ground of the papal
documents Wright covered, whether this is the tendency of the papal
documents or of Wright's interpretation of them. It certainly seems the
popes were conscious that they were writing in an Age of Nationalism
and adapted themselves to it.

[26] Since Wright gives examples of nationalism from other nations,
this omission seems to imply that he holds that there has been no exces-
sive nationalism in America. All in all, one notes in Wright's book the
tendency (which, since Vatican II, has been increasingly spotted as
"triumphalism") to absolve Catholicism, particularly the hierarchy,
from all charges of excess or defect in the matter of nationalism. The
tone of his book, thus, is much like the statements of the American
Catholic hierarchy as contrasted with the statements of the National
Council of Churches in Sister M. Janelle Cahoon's *Tensions and Dilemmas Facing Organized Christianity in the Contemporary United States
as Recognized in Official Church Statements* (Fordham University,
unpublished doctoral dissertation, 1963). In contrast to the latter,
Catholic statements, in the opinion of the present writer, were much
more lacking in self-criticism and given to "triumphalism."

[27] Gordon C. Zahn, *In Solitary Witness: The Life and Death of Franz
Jagerstatter* (New York: Holt, Rinehart, and Winston, 1964).

28 *Commonweal*, May 22, 1964, pp. 253–256.

29 *Ibid.*, p. 256.

30 The question can be raised: Does one properly talk about nationalism in American Catholicism, or nationalism among American Catholics? Actually, it seems to this writer that the latter implies the former. Since it can be argued that there cannot be a religion that is culture-free (see, for example, H. Richard Niebuhr, "Christ against Culture," in Schneider, *op. cit.*), it follows that, if nationalism is present among American Catholics, it must affect American Catholicism. The latter cannot exist as an abstraction apart from the society which produced it. And inevitably (if one follows the thesis developed by Karl Mannheim in *Ideology and Utopia*) even the questions asked and the issues treated in the most speculative theology show the mark of the culture in which they originate.

31 Guenter Lewy, *The Catholic Church and Nazi Germany* (New York: McGraw-Hill, 1964), p. xiii.

32 Peter Guilday, *The Life and Times of John Carroll* (New York: The Encyclopedia Press, 1922); Annabelle M. Melville, *John Carroll of Baltimore: Founder of the American Catholic Hierarchy* (New York: Scribner, 1955); John Gilmary Shea, *Life and Times of the Most Rev. John Carroll*, Vol. II of *History of the Catholic Church in the United States* (New York: Shea, 1888).

33 Melville, *op. cit.*, p. 286.

34 Upon his arrival in Charleston, Bishop England found he had only five priests, of whom only three had jurisdiction (Peter Guilday, *The Life and Times of John England* [2 vols., New York: The America Press, 1927], II, p. 481).

35 Peter Guilday, *ibid.*, I, p. viii. The biography of Guilday is the most comprehensive account of Bishop England's life published so far. Short biographical sketches of England are to be found in *The Works of the Right Rev. John England*, collected and arranged by the Right Rev. Ignatius A. Reynolds (5 vols.; Baltimore: Murphy, 1849). See also *The National Pastorals of the American Hierarchy (1792–1919)*, with a foreword, notes and index by Peter Guilday (Washington, D.C.: NCWC, 1923), and Peter Guilday, *A History of the Councils of Baltimore, 1791–1884* (New York: Macmillan, 1932). A new biography of England is needed, since Guilday's *Life*, written in the one-hundred-percent patriotic era of the 1920's, not only seems to exaggerate Bishop England's nationalism (for instance, the expression

"mystical love for America," seems to be more of a reflection of Guilday than a genuine reflection of Bishop England), but also seems to give, on occasion, inaccurate interpretations of Bishop England's writings. Thus, while it is true that in the long series of letters entitled *Domestic Slavery*, England maintained that Gregory XVI's Apostolic Brief on the Slave Trade did not refer to the American domestic institution of slavery, he did not claim, as Guilday has him do, that "far from condemning domestic slavery, the Holy Father endorsed it" (Guilday, *The Life* . . . , II, p. 472).

[36] *A Letter on the Moral Causes that Have Produced the Evil Spirit of the Times*: Addressed to the Honorable James Harper, Mayor of New York, including a Vindication of the Author from the Infamous Charges made against him by James Gordon Bennett, William L. Stone and Others (New York: J. Winchester, New World Press, 1844), p. 6. See also *The Complete Works of the Most Rev. John Hughes* (2 vols.; New York: Lawrence Kehoe, 1865); John R. G. Hassard, *Life of the Most Rev. John Hughes* (New York: Appleton, 1866); no author given, *The Life of Archbishop Hughes* (Philadelphia: T. B. Peterson, 1864).

[37] Richard J. Purcell, late Professor of History, The Catholic University of America. Quoted on the jacket of Moynihan's biography of Archbishop Ireland.

[38] The charge that there was an Americanist heresy was occasioned by the publication in France of Father Walter Elliott's biography of Father Isaac Hecker. While in the letter condemning the heresy, entitled *Testem Benevolentiae*, Leo XIII was careful not to accuse any American bishops of holding the doctrines he was condemning, Archbishop Ireland's adversaries interpreted the letter as a silencing of the Archbishop and a vindication of their point of view that he had gone too far in trying to accommodate Catholic teaching to the American scene. The Archbishop, for his part, continued to regard Americanism as a "phantom heresy." He wrote: "In Europe, Americanism was cradled as well as entombed; in America, it was unknown until it was condemned."—From *The Life of Archbishop Ireland*, p. 129, James Moynihan, copyrighted 1953 by Harper & Brothers, used by permission of the publishers.

[39] Archbishop John Ireland, *The Church and Modern Society* (St. Paul, Minn.: Pioneer Press, 1905); James H. Moynihan, *op. cit.*

[40] Allen Sinclair Will, *Life of Cardinal Gibbons: Archbishop of Baltimore* (2 vols.; New York: Dutton, 1922); John Tracy Ellis, *The Life of Cardinal Gibbons: Archbishop of Baltimore, 1834–1921* (2 vols.; Milwaukee, Wis.: Bruce, 1952). Ellis notes (*ibid.*, II, p. 659) that the Will's work "laid strong emphasis on the public career of the cardinal with proportionately more space devoted to his role as an American citizen than as a Catholic churchman." Certainly it is true (as will become obvious in subsequent chapters) that the Will's biography emphasizes Gibbons' patriotism; considering the era in which it was written, this could be dismissed simply as a reflection of the biographer's values more than of the subject's, were it not for the fact that Will, who had done an earlier biography of Gibbons which evidently met with the hearty approval of the Cardinal, was encouraged by him to write the more pretentious biography. Whether the nationalistic spirit reflected in the Will *Life*, published two years after the Cardinal's death, truly mirrors Gibbons himself seems to this present writer to be beside the point, since this evidently is the way in which the Cardinal wanted himself to be presented.

[41] Francis J. Spellman, *Action This Day* (New York: Scribner, 1943); *The Foundling* (New York: Scribner, 1951); *No Greater Love* (New York: Scribner, 1945); *Prayers and Poems* (New York: Scribner, 1946); *The Risen Soldier* (New York: Macmillan, 1944); *The Road to Victory* (New York: Scribner, 1942); *What America Means to Me* (New York: Scribner, 1953); Robert I. Gannon, S.J., *The Cardinal Spellman Story* (Garden City, N.Y.: Doubleday, 1962). The circular letters sent over his signature to the priests and people of the New York Archdiocese also provide information and insights into Cardinal Spellman's possible nationalism.

[42] This writer is happy to express her appreciation to Professor Robert Cross, Chairman of the Department of History, Columbia University, for suggesting Bishop John Lancaster Spalding as the member of the Catholic hierarchy who, in the last century during the nationalities' controversy—while he usually went along with the liberal position—successfully avoided the other horn of the dilemma, and did not, like his friend Archbishop Ireland, reject foreign nationalism in the American Church, only to fall prey to American nationalism.

Bishop McQuaid of Rochester and Archbishop Corrigan of New York are generally viewed as providing a contrast to the standpoint of

Cardinal Gibbons and Archbishop Ireland, since both Bishop McQuaid and Archbishop Corrigan disagreed heartily with their liberal views. However, in the matter of nationalism, the present writer agrees with Professor Cross that the so-called conservatives were no more aware of the pitfalls than the liberals. For an instance of Bishop McQuaid's nationalism, see Chapter 6, footnote 45.

[43] Hans Kohn, *American Nationalism*, p. 5, seems to concur in the opinion he quotes that "The intellectual leader of American Catholicism during the late nineteenth century was John Lancaster Spalding, Bishop of Peoria, and the twentieth century Catholicism has not produced his counterpart." Richard Hofstadter, *Anti-Intellectualism in American Life*, seems to see Bishop Spalding as a bright spot in what was otherwise an intellectual Catholic waste. He quotes the Peoria prelate, at the Third Plenary Council of Baltimore, when he urged the establishment of a Catholic University: "the ecclesiastical seminary is not a school of intellectual culture, either here in America or elsewhere, and to imagine that it can become the instrument of intellectual culture is to cherish a delusion" (p. 139).

[44] David Francis Sweeney, *The Life of John Lancaster Spalding* (New York: Herder and Herder, 1966).

[45] Curti, *op. cit.*, pp. 205–206.

[46] John Tracy Ellis, *John Lancaster Spalding: First Bishop of Peoria: American Educator* (Milwaukee, Wis.: Bruce, 1961); this is a published version of the Gabriel Richard Lecture for 1961 and is necessarily a brief treatment of the accomplishments of Bishop Spalding. John Lancaster Spalding's works include: *Essays and Reviews* (New York: Catholic Publ. Society, 1877); *Glimpses of Truth* (Chicago: McClurg, 1903); *Lectures and Discourses* (New York: Catholic Publication Society, 1882); *Opportunity and Other Essays and Addresses* (Chicago: McClurg, 1901); *The Religious Mission of the Irish People* (6th ed.; New York: Christian Press Association, 1897); *Socialism and Labor* (Chicago: McClurg, 1902); *Thoughts and Theories of Life and Education* (Chicago: McClurg, 1910).

[47] Lawrence J. Kenny, S.J., *The Catholic Mind*, XXV, 17, Sept. 8, 1927, pp. 321–339. Reprinted by permission.

[48] Kohn, *American Nationalism*, p. 26, quoting Michael Forrest, *Travels Through America* (Philadelphia: Johnson & Justice, 1793), p. 11.

[49] Kohn, *loc. cit.*

⁵⁰ Guilday, *The Life and Times of John Carroll*, p. 13.

⁵¹ It is interesting to note that when Hughes gave a lecture on "The Influence of Christianity on Social Servitude," March 29, 1843 (*Complete Works of Hughes*, I, pp. 371–385), England was the villain of the piece. No mention of slavery in the United States was made.

In the writings of Bishop England, the anti-British note is struck repeatedly. For instance, he mentions how the English anti-slavery society wanted to "rivet the chains of the white slaves in Ireland" while hypocritically "abolishing the slavery of the negroes in the West Indies" —thus causing trouble for American slave-holders in the South. *Works of England*, III, p. 113.

⁵² In point of fact, Archbishop Hughes in a sermon preached in the Hall of the House of Representatives, on Sunday, December 12, 1847, referred to George Washington as a "great man, who approached in the order of social and political excellence as near obedience to the Saviour's precept as man could approach" (*Christianity the Only Source of Moral, Social and Political Regeneration* [New York: Dunigan, 1848]).

As a young seminarian, only recently arrived in America, Hughes wrote a poem, *To the Home of My Fathers*, which included the following stanza:

"Is no Washington near thee, thou captive of ages,
    To marshall thy brave ones and lead them to war?
Is no Franklin arrayed in the list of thy sages?
    In that of thy heroes, no young Bolivar?"
                                                    —Hassard, *op. cit.*, p. 40.

⁵³ John Talbot Smith, *History of the Catholic Church in New York* (2 vols.; New York: Hall & Locke, 1905), I, p. 128.

⁵⁴ Guilday, *The Life and Times of John England*, II, p. 8, quoting Maguire, *The Irish in America*.

⁵⁵ Guilday, *ibid.*, p. 9, quoting the *Miscellany* for March 24, 1824.

⁵⁶ Herberg, *Protestant-Catholic-Jew*, p. 146.

⁵⁷ Sean O'Faolain, *King of the Beggars: A Life of Daniel O'Connell* (New York: Viking, 1938); William Shannon, *The American Irish* (New York: Macmillan, 1963), p. 21, writes: "Unless he [O'Connell] could marry the Church to the nationalist movement, he knew he had little chance of success."

⁵⁸ Extract from a sketch in the *Dublin Catholic Directory*, in *The Works of England*, I, p. 3.

⁵⁹ In this memoir of William George Read (*The Works of England*,

I, p. 8), the author notes that Bishop England was counteracting the dangerous principles of the French Revolution. Guilday insists that Bishop England was not the editor of the *Chronicle*, but its chief trustee (*Life*, I, pp. 457–458).

[60] Hughes, *The Church and the World* (New York: Dunigan, 1850), pp. 23–31.

[61] *Complete Works of Hughes*, II, p. 136.

[62] The present writer recalls hearing Cardinal Spellman, at a showing of a movie (on the work of Catholic Relief Services in Vietnam) to a group of Catholic editors in the spring of 1956, speak informally of his own two loves: love of his religion and love of America. Lately returned from a trip to the Far East, he told about reading in the newspaper of one of the cities he visited an article derogatory of America and critical of its good intentions. With tears in his eyes, he asked: How can they do this to us? How can they doubt the goodness of America?

[63] From *Protestant-Catholic-Jew* by Will Herberg, pp. 146–147. Copyright © 1955, 1960 by Will Herberg. Reprinted by permission of Doubleday & Co., Inc.

[64] James P. Shannon, "The Irish Catholic Immigration," in McAvoy, *Roman Catholicism and the American Way of Life*, p. 206: "In their celebrated fight to refuse the rule and the religion of England the Irish people identified the Catholic religion so closely with the Irish nation that the two have been synonymous in popular speech ever since."

As a participant in a procession with an Irish pilgrimage to Lourdes in 1954, the present writer personally witnessed an example of this union of nationalism and religion among the Irish. Every time the stanza of the Lourdes' hymn was sung in which the line occurs, "Be England thy dowry as 'twas in days of yore," the Irish pilgrims sang out, "Be Ireland thy dowry . . ." even though, by so doing, they were actually implying, in the context of the stanza, that it was Ireland— not England—that had been lost to the Faith! Quite obviously, of course, these Irish people were not considering literal implications. Neither, probably, were they denying the universal, supra-national implications of Christianity—at least, consciously or volitionally. The explanation for their conduct seems to lie rather in the (for them) inextricable intertwining of the symbols of nationalism with the common religion.

[65] John Higham, *Strangers in the Land: Patterns of American Nativism, 1860–1925* (New Brunswick, N.J.: Rutgers Univ. Press, 1955), p. 4, notes that while the word itself was coined around 1840, the spirit of American nativism appeared long before that date and was operative long after the word had dropped out of common parlance. In fact so early did the spirit of nativism appear in the life of the infant republic that it is contended that it was responsible for the passage of the Alien and Sedition Acts which were directed at least partially against Catholics.

[66] Guilday, *The Life and Times of John Carroll,* p. 720.

[67] *Ibid.,* p. 66. This figure is Guilday's own estimate based on Carroll's figures.

[68] So attuned did they feel to American life and national values, that they often felt themselves to be able to identify with other (native) Americans in a way impossible for immigrants from other foreign countries. Bishop England, for instance, fighting French influence in the American Church, argued that the Irish were more attuned to America than were the French. Guilday, *Life and Times of John England,* I, p. 481.

[69] *Ibid.,* pp. 364–365. Whether or not Bishop England was wholly correct in his explanation of anti-Catholicism, there is evidence to substantiate his view that the hostility was directed against *Irish* Catholics, and not just *foreign* Catholics in general. In the nativist riots in Philadelphia in the 1840's, when Catholic churches were burned, they were churches with Irish congregations, German Catholic Churches in the same area escaping unscathed. See Carl Frederick Wittke, *The Irish in America* (Baton Rouge: Louisiana State University, 1956).

[70] Ray Allen Billington, *The Protestant Crusade 1800–1860: A Study of the Origins of American Nativism* (New York: Macmillan, 1938), p. 89.

[71] *Ibid.,* p. 73.

[72] *Ibid.,* p. 86.

[73] *Ibid.,* p. 88.

[74] *Ibid.,* p. 108.

[75] *Ibid.,* p. 181.

[76] *Ibid.,* p. 157. The Catholics had protested that the public schools were, in effect, Protestant, and that Catholic children in such schools were forced to use Protestant bibles.

[77] *Ibid.*, p. 312.

[78] *Ibid.*, p. 118.

[79] *National Pastorals of the American Hierarchy.*

[80] Higham, *op. cit.*, p. 4.

[81] *Ibid.*, p. 178.

[82] Hassard, *op. cit.*, p. 145: "It would not be easy to overrate the reputation which Father Hughes acquired by his triumphant vindication of the Catholic faith. Vilification of Catholics was just then in fashion all over the United States . . . In Pennsylvania the Catholic Church had so far found no defender able to grapple with her adversaries and fight them in a fair field . . . When Mr. Hughes stood forth, the faithful soon felt that a strong arm was striking blows for them, and henceforth they looked to him whenever they were attacked." Hassard comments (pp. 156–158) on the strong language used on both sides in the debate, which was considerably modified by mutual consent when the speeches were prepared for publication.

[83] Hassard, *op. cit.*, p. 276.

[84] Kohn, *American Nationalism*, p. 144.

[85] Curti, *op. cit.*, p. 77. Guilday, *Life and Times of John England*, II, p. 195, gives long excerpts from Morse's writings.

[86] Billington, *op. cit.*, p. 388.

[87] *Loc. cit.*

[88] Herberg, *Protestant-Catholic-Jew*, p. 146.

[89] John Higham, in a perceptive article "Another Look at Nativism," *The Catholic Historical Review*, XLIV, 2, July 1958, pp. 147–158, gives reasons for the particular hostility which the Irish immigrants attracted. Higham notes that the Irish were climbing the social ladder faster than the Germans. The latter were relatively static, since the sons of German immigrants were more content to follow in the place of their fathers. Furthermore, the Irish were concentrated in occupations where they were exposed to the competitive intrusion of new nationalities; they were thus *driven* upward to escape identification with their less American rivals.

For further insights into the operations of nativism, *see* the article by Colman J. Barry, O.S.B., "Some Roots of American Nativism," pp. 137–146, in the same issue of *The Catholic Historical Review*.

[90] Higham, *Strangers in the Land*, has a reproduction of a cartoon by Thomas Nast about which Higham comments: "Thomas

Nast, America's leading political cartoonist, created perhaps the most terrifying anti-Catholic drawing in our history. A part of his assault on Tammany Hall, it shows Boss Tweed (leaning on edge of cliff) and Irish politicians collaborating in destruction of American public school system." The children pushed from the cliff fall to the shore to which are swimming foreign invaders, whose mitres form the snapping jaws of crocodiles.

[91] Moynihan, *op. cit.*, p. 48.

Donald L. Kinzer in *An Episode in Anti-Catholicism: the American Protective Association* (Seattle: University of Washington Press, 1964), p. 249, remarks that it is "rather unfair to say that 'the APA movement' was of no importance in United States history, but the American Protective Association as a secret lodge scarcely rippled the surface of its times . . . pursued a brief career of distrust and suspicion, and died for no apparent reason other than that the times were not ripe for them to flourish."

[92] Gibbons, "Patriotism and Politics," *North American Review*, CCIV (April, 1892), p. 392, as quoted by Curti, *op. cit.*, p. 184.

A final footnote to this brief sketch of nativism as one of the background factors in the production of American Catholic nationalism is provided by the comment with which Higham ends his discussion of the "closing of the gates" to free immigration as a result of post-World War I nativism. He writes (p. 330): "the new equation between national loyalty and a large measure of political and social conformity would long outlive the generation that established it." Perhaps it is one of the greater ironies in the American Catholic reaction to nativism that (if such authors as Daniel Bell, Daniel Moynihan, and William Shannon are right in their assessment of Catholic political conservatism particularly in the post-McCarthy era) Catholics indeed did end up adopting nativist principles, and the equation between loyalty and conformity is still with us.

[93] The exception among the liberals was Bishop Spalding who expressed his cultural pluralist position in an introduction to P. M. Abbelen, *Venerable Mother M. Caroline Friess* (St. Louis, 1893); see Cross, *op. cit.*, p. 252, note 4.

[94] Cross, *ibid.*, p. 90.

[95] Guilday, *Life and Times of John Carroll*, p. 292.

[96] *Ibid.*, p. 423 ff.

[97] *Ibid.*, p. 724.

[98] Guilday, *Life and Times of John England*. Another example of dissension among nationality groups occurred when Du Bois, chosen as Bishop of New York, had to vindicate his Americanism against the Irish (*ibid.*, II, p. 448).

[99] Cross, *op. cit.*, p. 93.

[100] Moynihan, *op. cit.*, pp. 62–63, quoting correspondence between Ireland and Gibbons. Nevertheless, in an article in *The Irish Ecclesiastical Record*, Cardinal Gibbons expressed the sentiment that, in America, the interests of the Catholic religion in "this age are largely bound up with the interests of the Irish people" (Ellis, *Life of Gibbons*, I, p. 383).

[101] Ireland, *The Church and Modern Society*.

[102] *The Question of Nationality in its Relation to the Catholic Church in the United States*, pp. 44–45, as quoted by Colman J. Barry, O.S.B., *The Catholic Church and German Americans* (Washington, D.C.: The Catholic University, 1953), p. 84.

[103] Barry, *op. cit.*, p. 80.

[104] *Ibid.*, p. 116.

[105] Cross, *op. cit.*, Chapter V; Moynihan, *op. cit.*, Chapter IV. Barry, *op. cit.*, successfully defends Cahensly from the charge that he was a tool of the Prussian government.

[106] Moynihan, *op. cit.*, p. 70; Ellis, *Life of Gibbons*, I, p. 373.

[107] Barry, *op. cit.*, p. 173. Father Barry quotes the words of Father Francis Goller as characteristic of these German leaders who believed "that the United States was a country but not yet a nation."

[108] See p. 104 above.

[109] Certain "unintended consequences" of the victory of the side represented by Archbishop Ireland in the American Church should be noted as perhaps not unrelated to the issue of American nationalism. Both Richard Hofstadter (*Anti-Intellectualism in American Life*, p. 138) and Colman Barry, O.S.B. (in "The German Catholic Immigrant" in McAvoy, *Roman Catholicism and the American Way of Life*) suggest that the anti-intellectualism of the Catholic Church in America is due in no small measure to the dominance of the Irish-American group which (according to Hofstadter) allowed the American Church to absorb "little of the impressive scholarship of German Catholicism or the questioning intellectualism of the French Church." Father Barry,

noting that the record of German Catholic contributions has been limited, suggests that too hasty Americanization was a serious cause. "Another area [of study] that awaits the historian of intellectual and religious life is the nature and character of American Catholic spirituality, or interior life, which has not been touched as yet. Why has there been a slow and reluctant response to the ideals of community worship, of the liturgical movement, of a respect for the Catholic traditions of participation, singing and a Scriptural-centered life? Were immigrant groups such as the Germans swept into the dominant current of the 'American' secular cultural patterns?" (*Ibid.*, pp. 202–203)

The possible relationship of anti-intellectualism and uncritical nationalism will be given consideration later in this study.

It should be noted that the difference in tradition influenced the Irish and the German Catholic immigrants to the United States to take different stands upon the matter of parochial versus public schools. The Irish, with their tradition of anti-intellectualism, were quite willing, at first, to accept the public schools. It was not until they objected to the public schools as being inculcators of Protestantism that they opted for parochial schools. (It was not until the Third Plenary Council that the bishops demanded the establishment of parochial schools.) The Germans, on the other hand, being used to Catholic and Lutheran schools in Germany, chose to continue the parochial schools in America.

# 4/"How Catholic America Is"

*. . . Without the design of any man, our land was named America in honor of one of God's saints, Emeric or Amerigo, who died rich in merits in far-off Hungary, but whose name means self-government or Liberty; . . . a Christ-bearer discovered the land; . . . he found it through the Cross; . . . the arms of Mary protected him in his work. Surely the newborn land, over which Heaven took such care, is meant for glorious days.*[1]

*To Spain, when her Catholicity was her life, this nation owes her birth . . . ; to old Catholic France, her emancipation from servitude to a foreign state.*[2]

Considering the one-hundred-per-cent Americanism of the 1920's during which the above paragraphs were written, their sentiments are not very surprising. Catholic historians today, however, do not need to take an exaggerated view of the Church's place in American history; indeed, the attempt of prelates and other apologists in the past to prove "how Catholic America is," and to show that all that is good in the American system derives from Catholic origins, fills them with embarrassment. Perhaps it is as much a mark of the emotional security of Catholics today in being fully accepted Americans, as it is a tribute to the scholarship of present-day Catholic historians, that, in the words of one of their number, they can give a "far more realistic view of the Catholic place in the development of the United States."[3]

It is understandable that, throughout the nineteenth century, Catholics who were, for the most part, recent immigrants to American shores should have embroidered tales which would at once show the ideological debt the United States owed Catholicism and the practical obligations which Americans in general owed Catholics in particular for the independence of the thirteen colonies and the formation of the United States. Referring to such legends, Guilday writes:

Many of these legends bear the stamp of their origin, namely, as over-zealous enthusiasm to claim as much of the glory as possible; others are subtle and require historical disproof. Among these is the oft-quoted story that it was through Father John Carroll that the Pope used his influence to induce King Louis of France to aid America. This claim, entirely fictitious, is part of the general traditional belief that John Carroll had aided Jefferson in drafting the Declaration of Independence. The climax of these popular legends is the one which reports that King George III refused to sign the Catholic Emancipation Bill (1829) because of his hatred for John Carroll. "He detached America from my dominions by the aid of the French army and navy, and the force of the Irish Catholics"—such is the supposed speech of the king to Pitt! *Nimis probans, nihil probans.* The truth is that Father John Carroll took no active part in the Revolution, apart from his invitation by the Continental Congress to accompany the American Commissioners to Quebec.[4]

Evidently Carroll himself—even under the provocation of anti-Catholic articles which claimed that the United States was an exclusively Protestant nation whose culture was a product of purely Protestant arts and sciences—did not exaggerate his, or any other Catholic's, part in the struggle for independence. In an article published in the *United States Gazette* of June 10, 1789 (answering an attack, published the month previously, against Catholic office-holding), Carroll asked: "Can we so soon forget that the bitterest enemies of our national prosperity profess the same religion which prevails generally in the United States?" But, as his biographer remarks, "He did not voice the obvious corollary that it was a Catholic power, France, which had made possible the victory at Yorktown."[5]

Moreover, instead of trying to prove (as we shall see some of his successors tried) that it was the *Catholic*, rather than the Protestant, religion which was the more favorable to freedom, Carroll was content to show that no sect or branch of religion could make that claim, while "the neglect or contempt of no one body of clergy would cause liberty or morality to expire."[6]

Without making any undue claims for Catholicism, the Baltimore prelate focussed, instead, on developing the theme of the consonance of American political institutions with Catholic theology. "Carroll came to personify the desire for complete compatibility of the ancient Church with the new state."[7] While he never failed to let his English friends know "how righteous he felt the American cause,"[8] he did this apparently without any of the over-defensiveness which characterizes those who are marked by secret doubts. While occasionally (for instance, in his adulation of Washington)[9] he seemed to express an exaggerated patriotism, on the whole, the tone of his writings is one of moderation. While he certainly took his Catholicism seriously and was quite confident of the merits and continued success of the American system, Archbishop Carroll apparently did not feel that proving the consonance of Catholicism and American political institutions depended on proving the origin of the latter in Catholicism. Unbeset with conflict himself over the place of Catholics in America, he indicated himself ready for the Church to face the experiences of the American scene, even when they were totally new to Catholic life and culture.[10] Himself at home in the United States, Archbishop Carroll evidently did not see why the Church could not be also.

The prelates who followed the Archbishop of Baltimore apparently did not feel so much at home; or, at least, they did not seem able to take their "home" so much for granted. After his time, a difference is to be noted that is sometimes subtle (for instance, in the case of Bishop England), that is, at other times, fairly obvious (for instance, in the case of Archbishop Hughes). Feeling themselves on the defensive, those prelates who succeeded Archbishop Carroll were no longer content simply to show the *congruence* of Catholicism and the American system of government; frequently they appear hard-pressed to show a more direct connection. In 1822, for instance, at the time of the foundation of the *Miscellany*, Bishop England declared in the prospectus that the paper would attempt an explanation of the doctrines of the Roman Catholic Church for those who "imagined they were contradicting Catholics, *when they held Catholic doctrines themselves*"[11] (emphasis supplied). Bishop England was repeatedly at pains to show, in his lectures and writings, the Catholic origin or Catholic identity of what his non-Catholic fellow citizens regarded as "American."

In his discourse upon the death of President William Harrison, Bishop England thus explained the origins of republicanism:

. . . Look through the records of the world, and see where the principles of true republicanism are first to be found. They had their origin in Christianity, and their earliest instance in the church of which we are members. Her institutions are eminently republican. Her rulers are chosen by the common consent, her officers are obliged to account strictly to those over whom they preside, her guide is a written constitution of higher force than the will of any individual. What call you this? Aristocracy? Monarchy? It is republicanism. Look again. Where were the bulwarks found that stayed the ravages of the barbarians of the North, when they devastated the south of Europe? In the republican Catholic States of Italy. Go to a nation still more familiar to you; search the pages of English history . . . The principles of the common law, that mighty fabric in which English liberty is said to reside, have been traced back to the Catholic Church. In this, then, is the germ of liberty to be found . . .[12]

In his address before Congress, delivered January 8, 1826, Bishop England spoke in the same vein, pointing out that Catholic Italy was a soil fertile in republics:

What was the religion of William Tell? He was a Roman Catholic. Look not only to the Swiss republics, but take San Marino,— this little state, during centuries, the most splendid specimen of the purest democracy, and this democracy protected by our Popes during these centuries . . .[13]

Bishop England, however, avoided the simplistic argumentation of some of the Catholic apologists who were to come after him, especially those who use the example of San Marino to prove that the republic is a Catholic form![14] In the same speech to Congress, while he takes pains to show that the greater number of republics are Catholic, Bishop England indicates that so also are the greater number of monarchies. "The fact is so for an obvious reason, because it is the religion of the great bulk of the civilized world."[15]

It is in the lectures and writings of Archbishop Hughes that the theme *how Catholic America is* reaches the breadth of its development. In a lecture entitled "The Catholic Chapter in the History of the United States," the New York prelate goes to such pains to trace the Catholic origins of the nation that his theme, in paraphrase, becomes: "America is really a Catholic phenomenon." Starting with the fact that the New World was discovered by a Catholic, Archbishop Hughes recounts Catholic participation in the founding of the nation. "During the contest, so far as religion is concerned, who were your allies and friends? I answer Catholics, and—if I may be permitted to add—none but Catholics."[16] He concludes his lecture:

What, then, is the meaning of the words Protestant country, as applied to the United States? I suppose that, at last, it will come down to signify nothing more than that the majority of the inhabitants are Protestants.[17]

In an article published in the *Metropolitan Magazine* in December, 1858, this same prelate stressed his belief in the Catholic derivation of American political institutions:

In the annals of Church history, there has never been a country which in its civil and social relations has exhibited so fair an opportunity for developing the practical harmonies of Catholic faith and of Catholic charity as the United States.

The great elements of our institutions, namely, representative government, electoral franchise, trial by jury, municipal polity, were all the inventions of Catholics alone.[18]

In the institution of the monastery, Archbishop Hughes saw the source of our constitutional government:

The very word 'community' was unknown before, and had its origin in those institutions (monasteries). Admirable schools of wisdom and justice and freedom too!—the essence of whose constitution and government has been infused into the best civil organizations of modern times![19]

And the inevitable mention of San Marino:

> . . . Before Columbus discovered the Western Continent there
> was a people in Europe acquainted with the rights and privileges
> of republican government . . . there was one little republic (San
> Marino) installed in the Papal States. How long? For fourteen
> hundred years she has continued to preserve her liberty . . .
>
> And now speaking to this republic, which is an enlargement of
> such a model, what should be the desire of every man who loved
> her? . . . That she may remain, preserving her liberty and the
> laws of justice and equality as long as the Republic of San Marino,
> and as great a century hence as she designs to aspire.[20]

Archbishop Hughes was not content to show the Catholic
origin of American political institutions. Speaking, October
19, 1840, on the school question, at a time when the Catholics
of New York were trying to get their share of funds of the
Public School Society which was actually a private association,
the prelate pointed up the Catholic derivation of various social
institutions as well as technological inventions used by Americans. He said:

> Who was the founder of Sunday-schools? It was Saint Charles
> Borromeo—a Catholic. In a word, there is no department of
> knowledge in which Catholics have not been distinguished. But to
> go further: who discovered a quicker means of communication than
> the railroad? It was not used so extensively in this country as in
> some others, but it might be important even here, if an invasion
> should be made of any part of our coast, to communicate informa-
> tion to Washington and receive an answer back in less time than it
> should be done by railroads. He would deserve a prize who should
> invent the means of sending information from Niagara to Wash-
> ington and receiving an answer back in six or seven hours. And
> yet the equivalent of this has been done by a Catholic priest who
> invented the telegraph. If they turned to music, who had brought it

to its present state by the perfection of instrumental music? Who had taught the canvas to speak? And who had given life and animation to the cold marble? Catholics. And all the boasted superiority of Protestants was yet an infinite distance from the productions of Catholics, and they were proud to distraction if they succeeded in producing a tolerable copy of that which Catholics had invented.[21]

In Hughes—so it seems to the present writer—the tendency in Catholic apologetics to defend Catholicism by showing "how Catholic America really is" reached its zenith. Certainly, as shall be indicated presently, attempts in a similar way to show the congruence of Catholicism and American institutions by using Catholicism as the norm are found in the writings and speeches of Archbishop Ireland and Cardinal Gibbons; usually, however, their attempts at congruence follow a different line.[22] For Archbishop Hughes, Catholicism had to be justified to America in terms of Catholicism itself. For him, Catholicism—and not Americanism—was the norm. Even when he was speaking for apologetical purposes (in the technical sense of the term "apologetics"), he was never apologetic about Catholicism in the sense that he made any kind of effort to render it especially congenial or connatural to American hearers. In this he differed remarkably from prelates who were to follow him, especially Archbishop Ireland and Cardinal Gibbons. Thus, his biographer Hassard remarked that there were three classes of Catholics whom Archbishop Hughes felt to be mischievous:

. . . the first were those of the Young Ireland stamp; the second, those which spoke perhaps unconsciously, as if they looked upon the Catholic Church in this country substantially as an Irish Church, or a German Church . . . and the third, as he supposed were trying to Americanize the Church by conforming Catholic

practices—so far as they could do so consistently with sound doctrine and good discipline—to the character of the American people.
I think he disliked the third class the most of the three . . .[23]

At the 1856 commencement exercises of St. John's College
(now Fordham University), Archbishop Hughes' disapproval
of this third class was rather markedly shown. In his address,
Orestes Brownson had remarked that, if the Catholic religion
could be presented through mediums and under auspices more
congenial to their feelings and habits, the progress of the
Church would be far greater than it had been. "At the close
of Dr. Brownson's address, he [Archbishop Hughes] went
upon the platform, and, vastly to the entertainment of the
audience, kindly but decidedly controverted the doctor's
opinions."[24]

It seems true then that, while Archbishop Hughes was
intent on justifying Catholicism to America, it had to be on
Catholicism's own terms. He made no conscious attempt to
"Americanize" Catholicism. Certainly his efforts to show
Americans how Catholic America really was stemmed from
his desire to have the Faith accepted; but it can be conjectured
whether or not those efforts proceeded also from a desire to
justify America to himself. For America would be justified
to this churchman only if he could show it to be really Catholic, truly in line with Catholicism itself.

For the most part, Cardinal Gibbons followed a different
method of showing the compatibility of American institutions
and Catholicism. In his writings and public discourses, however, he did occasionally point up the Catholic derivation of
American political and social institutions. Thus, he contributed a chapter entitled "The Claims of the Church in the
Making of the Republic," to John Gilmary Shea's *The Cross
and the Flag*. Expressing himself along the lines of the theme

that to the Catholic Church must be attributed all that was
done in the New World, the Cardinal wrote:

. . . that the children and members of the Catholic Church have
been, at all periods of our country's history, among its truest
friends, and are entitled to the proud distinction of being the founders and chief builders of that magnificent temple of liberty . . .[25]

In the introduction to the volume *The Retrospect of Fifty
Years* (which contained a collection of the Cardinal's previous
writings and major addresses), he claimed that to the Catholic
Church is owed a debt for consolidating into one people di-
verse nations with different, often hostile, points of view. To
Catholicism, too, is owed American liberty.

. . . many men once amongst us feared the Catholic Church because they thought her opposed to liberty; yet if they had read
history, even superficially, they would have known that no liberty
which they possessed has come to them except through the agency
of that religion which molded our barbarian ancestors into the
civilized nations of Europe. But for her there would have been no
civilization today, and without civilization there could have been
no liberty.[26]

Gibbons here reiterated the sentiments he expressed at
length in his book, *Our Christian Heritage*; particularly in the
chapter entitled "The Religious Element in Our American
Civilization."[27]

Archbishop Ireland, too, on occasion was wont to empha-
size that the Catholic Church was and "is a great power in
the land, and an important factor in shaping the destinies of
the Commonwealth."[28] In an address entitled "The Catholic
Church and Civil Society," he was intent on showing the origin
of American ideas of civil liberty in the works of Thomas

Aquinas, Suarez, and Bellarmine.[29] Elsewhere in the same lecture, he said:

> The Church fought the battles of personal liberty against slavery and serfdom. It was by her Pontiffs and her councils that the "rights of man" were made known to the world. Her dogma of a common brotherhood struck to the ground the manacles that heartless man was always too willing to impose upon his weaker fellow. No social law or feudal caste could long resist the example of the great Church . . .[30]

In another address, entitled "The Church and the Age," delivered on the occasion of the Silver Jubilee of the episcopal consecration of Cardinal Gibbons, Archbishop Ireland again emphasized the Catholic origin of American democratic ideals.

> The age of democracy! The Catholic Church, I am sure, has no fear of democracy, this flowering of her own most sacred principles of the equality, fraternity, and liberty of all men, in Christ and through Christ. These principles are found upon every page of the gospel. From the moment they were first confided to the Church they have been ceaselessly leavening minds and hearts towards the full recognition of the rights and the dignity of man, towards the elevation of the multitude, and the enjoyment of freedom from unnecessary restrictions . . . The whole history of the Catholic Church is the record of the enfranchisement of the slave, the curbing of the tyranny of kings, the defense of the poor, of woman, of all the people . . . The great theologians of the Church lay the foundations of political democracy which today attains its perfect form . . .[31]

Thus, for Archbishop Ireland, American democracy is the fruit of a Catholic tree. While both Cardinal Gibbons and Archbishop Ireland on certain occasions and in some of their writings, as has been illustrated, were inclined to bring out "how Catholic America really is," on the whole, however, they turned their attention in a different direction and used their energies to demonstrate to their fellow citizens—Catholic and non-Catholic alike—how *American* Catholicism is. Unlike Archbishop Hughes, these two prelates not only approved of efforts to render Catholicism more agreeable to the American mind, but exerted themselves to make the very adaptations which had evoked the hearty disapproval of Archbishop Hughes. Like the New York prelate, Archbishop Ireland and Cardinal Gibbons were intent on justifying Catholicism to America, but increasingly they did it on *American* terms. This became the norm of their endeavor. And it may be asked with a certain justice—considering their recorded lectures, writings, and the presentation of their lives by their biographers—in their efforts to make Catholicism conform completely to American life, did they, in a strange abandonment of the prophetic function of religion, put the Church under the judgment of the *nation*?

More than an incidental difference between Archbishop Hughes, on the one side, and Archbishop Ireland and Cardinal Gibbons, on the other, is symbolized by the fact that, while Hughes boasted that he had voted only once in his life, both Ireland and Gibbons publicized the fact that they never neglected voting; they urged it as an obligation on all churchmen. This was part of their effort to establish the *American* character of the Catholic Church and of its hierarchy. The documentation of their efforts to show "how American the Church is" is the work of the next chapter.[32]

*NOTES*

[1] Kenny, "America—a Land of Destiny," *The Catholic Mind* (Sept. 8, 1927) p. 324.
[2] *Ibid.*, p. 334.

[3] Henry J. Browne, "Catholicism in the United States," in James Ward Smith and A. Leland Jamison, *The Shaping of American Religion*, Princeton, N.J.: Princeton University Press), Vol. I, pp. 72–121.

[4] Guilday, *Life and Times of John Carroll*, pp. 90–91.

[5] Melville, *John Carroll of Baltimore*, pp. 87, 88.

[6] *Ibid.*

[7] Browne, *op. cit.*, p. 78.

[8] *Ibid.*

[9] Melville, *op. cit.*, pp. 168–169, 309. In the new nation, this veneration of Washington was common, as Lipset shows (*The First New Nation*, p. 22). Lipset is at pains to indicate that the presence of a charismatic leader like Washington is a functional requirement for the establishment of national authority in a new nation.

[10] In fact, according to Melville (*op. cit.*, p. 138), Archbishop Carroll wanted to send boys preparing for the priesthood to the ordinary secular colleges springing up throughout the thirteen states.

[11] Guilday, *Life and Times of John England*, I, p. 456.

[12] *Ibid.*, II, p. 43.

[13] *Works of England*, IV, p. 185.

[14] Father Isaac Hecker, for one, later used the same examples as England, but with much less intellectual discrimination. To quote from Hecker's *The Church and the Age* (New York: Catholic World, 1887): ". . . all republics since the Christian era have sprung into existence under the influence of the Catholic Church" (p. 84). "During its three centuries of existence a republican form of government has nowhere under Protestant ascendency made its appearance" (p. 71). "There exists a necessary bond and relation between the truths contained in the Declaration of Independence and the revealed truths of Christianity . . ." (p. 79). "The course of Europe was that of negation; the course of the United States was that of affirmation . . . Europe, under the lead of the religious revolution of the 16th century, turned its back on Catholicity and entered upon the downward road that ends in death; the republic of the United States . . . started in the 18th century with its face to Catholicity, and is in the ascending way of life to God" (pp. 96–97). Chapter II of this volume, entitled "Relation of Church and State in America," has as its sub-title, "The Principles of American Freedom are Catholic—Protestantism is Opposed to Them."

[15] *Works of England, loc. cit.*

[16] Hughes, *The Catholic Chapter in the History of the United States* (New York: Dunigan, 1852), p. 14.

[17] *Ibid.*, p. 34.

[18] Hassard, *Life of Hughes*, p. 349.

[19] *Works of Hughes*, I, p. 359.

[20] *Ibid.*, II, p. 132.

[21] *Ibid.*, I, p. 119.

[22] This will be demonstrated in the next chapter.

[23] Hassard, *op. cit.*, p. 383.

[24] *Ibid.*

[25] John Gilmary Shea, *The Cross and the Flag* (New York: Catholic Historical League of America, 1899), p. 75.

[26] Will, *Life of Cardinal Gibbons*, II, p. 903.

[27] Ellis, *The Life of Cardinal Gibbons*, II, p. 527.

[28] Ireland, *op. cit.*, p. 9.

[29] *Ibid.*, pp. 28–31.

[30] *Ibid.*, p. 37.

[31] *Ibid.*, p. 99.

[32] The reader will be aware—as is the present writer—that the analytical distinction between the concept, "how Catholic America is," and the concept, "how American the Church is," is useful mainly for establishing a trend in the relationship of the Catholic Church to America and the emergence of nationalism in American Catholicism. Needless to say, it is not clearly evident in a particular passage that the writer's argumentation is based on one or the other concept. For instance, is the following passage from Brownson (quoted from the *American Republic*, p. 97 of Alvan S. Ryan, *The Brownson Reader*, New York: Kenedy, 1935) clearly a reflection of one or the other: "Neither the state nor the people, elsewhere than in the United States, can understand practically such separation (of church and state) . . . But this is no where possible out of the United States, for no where else is the state organized on catholic principles, or capable of acting . . . in harmony with a really catholic church."

# 5/"How American the Church Is"

*"The religion of patriotism is not sufficiently under-
stood, and yet it is this religion that gives to country
its majesty, and to patriotism its sacredness and force."*[1]

Archbishop Ireland was, in his day, considered an eloquent
man, and the sentence quoted above is typical of the flights
of oratory for which he was famous. It was in a discourse on
patriotism delivered before the New York Commandery of the
Loyal Legion, April 4, 1894, that he thus expressed himself.
In his mention of "the religion of patriotism," Archbishop
Ireland seems to have come perilously close to "the overarching religion" which Herberg would decry some sixty years
later as being the religion of the nation unthinkingly accepted
by religious Americans. Of course, one would be hard put to
prove that Archbishop Ireland had actually accepted the phenomenon which Herberg, later on, was to analyze. Certainly
in his writings and speeches as a bishop of the Catholic
Church, even when he lacked theological precision,[2] Archbishop Ireland never claimed that country came before God;
in fact, in the same speech on patriotism he gave as the order
of allegiances: God first; next to God, country.[3] However, it
is evident that, whatever may have been his private strictures

on the subject, from his writings, speeches and the correspondence to which his biographer makes us privy, no thought on
the possibility that there could be conflict in these two allegiances ever crossed the Archbishop's mind in public. So much
of an ecclesiastical Theodore Roosevelt in personality, he
seems to have shared Roosevelt's inability to see that a stand
taken by his country could be other than righteous.[4] Intent
on educing the support of religion for American patriotism,
Archbishop Ireland was apparently equally intent to show how
well his Catholicism fitted in with his Americanism. The
attempt to prove the congruence of Catholicism and American
institutions, which had started in the days of Archbishop John
Carroll, became, in the days of the somewhat blustery urbanity
of Archbishop John Ireland, an attempt to convince his fellow
citizens how positively American the Catholic Church had
become.

## "AS MUCH INDEPENDENCE AS POSSIBLE FOR THE AMERICAN CHURCH"

The effort of the American hierarchy to prove the compatibility of the two social institutions—the Church and the
American nation—had begun with John Carroll. In fact, his
biographer Guilday is at pains to show that so early in his
career did he understand the requirements of American patriotism for the cleric that "he was the first priest of the rebellious colonies to refuse obedience to the last of the superiors,
Father John Lewis, who acted all through the war as Vicar-
General of the London district."[5] Whether or not Guilday is
right in implying that Carroll's refusal to recognize the authority of Father Lewis proceeded from patriotism—certainly
there is reason to believe that Carroll thought Lewis no longer
had jurisdiction over the colonies—it does seem evident that

Carroll wanted the Church in America to be free of any ties
to England.[6] Looking toward the newly-established American
government as one "from whose influence America anticipates
all the blessings of justice, peace, plenty, good order and civil
and religious liberty,"[7] before his selection as bishop was
approved by the Holy See, John Carroll went to great pains
to assure that the Catholic Church in America would adapt
its organization to something more in keeping with the American form of government. As a consequence he was not slow
to petition the Vatican that as much independence as possible
be given the American Church.[8] Particularly did he urge that
the Church in America be freed from all foreign jurisdiction.[9]
The desire to have the organization of the Church accord with
American ideas of fittingness made Carroll and his priests
hesitate at first over the question of the establishment of the
hierarchy in America.[10] However, even though they did not
want a bishop, the appointment of a temporary superior
dependent on Propaganda was even less to their liking.[11]

After John Carroll had been consecrated bishop, "a con-
stant theme of his episcopate was the consonance of American
political institutions with Catholic theology."[12] Mindful of
the need to attract to the American mission field priests who
would understand America,[13] Carroll realized that

the future greatness of the Church of God in the United States lay
in teaching her children that the needs and aspirations of the
nation were all in consonance with Catholic doctrines and Catholic
principles.[14]


## "TO MAKE THE CHURCH IN AMERICA THROB
## WITH AMERICAN LIFE"

John Carroll's biographer, Guilday, paid tribute to the
prelate's success in keeping the Catholic Church in America
free from foreign entanglements when he wrote that

it will ever be said to his high honour among the prelates of the past that he handed on to his successors an ecclesiastical establishment which saw America with American eyes and spoke of America in terms understood by the American people.[15]

If Archbishop Carroll conceived of his mission as one of assuring that the Catholic Church be established in the recently created United States as an indigenous institution, Archbishop John Ireland evidently conceived of his mission, approximately one hundred years later, as one of insuring the continued American character of a Church whose numbers swelled with practically every boat-load of immigrants. At the centenary commemoration of the establishment of the American hierarchy, Archbishop Ireland spoke thus:

> There is danger: we receive large accessions of Catholics from foreign countries. God witnesses that they are welcome. I will not intrude on their personal affections and tastes; but these, if foreign, shall not encrust themselves upon the Church. Americans have no longing for a Church with a foreign aspect; they will not submit to its influence. Only institutions to the manor born prosper; exotics have but sickly forms.
>
> America treats us well; her flag is our protection. Patriotism is a Catholic virtue. I would have Catholics be the first patriots in the land . . . There are occasions without number when Catholics, as citizens, can prove their patriotism; and of such occasions they should be eager to avail themselves. The men most devoted to the institutions of the country, the most ardent lovers of its flag, should be they who believe in Catholic truth, who breathe the air of Catholic sanctuaries.[16]

Tenaciously insisting that the American character of the Church in the United States be preserved, and that clergy and laity alike participate actively as American citizens[17] (Ireland had expressed the sentiments that the non-voter deserved exile[18]), he was fully in accord with the American sense of mission as it had been developed by the most extravagant of American patriots.[19] In one oration he proclaimed:

In the course of history Providence selects now one nation, now another to be the guide and the exemplar of humanity's progress . . . A great era, the like of which has not been seen, is now dawning upon the horizon. Which will now be God's chosen nation to guide the destinies of mankind?

The chosen nation of the future! She is before my soul's vision. Giant in stature, buoyant in the freshness of morning youth, matronly in prudent stepping, the ethereal breezes of liberty caressing with loving touch her tresses, she is—no one seeing her can doubt it—the queen, the mistress, the teacher of coming ages. To her keeping the Creator has entrusted a mighty continent, whose shores two oceans lave, rich in all nature's gifts, imbosoming precious and useful minerals, fertile in soil, salubrious in air, beauteous in vesture, the fair region of His predilection, which He had held in reserve for long centuries, awaiting the propitious moment in humanity's evolution to bestow it on men, when men were worthy to possess it . . . Of this nation it is the mission to give forth a new humanity. She embodies in her life and her institutions the hopes, the ambitions, the dreamings of humanity's priests and prophets. To her daring in the race of progress, to her devotion at the shrine of liberty, there is no limit. Peace and prosperity spread over her their sheltering wings.

The nation of the future! Need I name it? Your hearts quiver loving it.[20]

And in another speech he thus proclaimed America's mission and his own loyalty to it:

Republic of America, receive from me the tribute of my love and my loyalty. With my whole soul I do thee homage. I pray from my heart that thy glory be never dimmed—*Esto perpetua.* Thou bearest in thy hands the hopes of the human race. Thy mission from God is to show to nations that men are capable of highest civil and political liberty. Be thou ever free and prosperous. Through thee may liberty triumph over the earth from the rising to the setting sun!—*Esto perpetua . . .* Believe me, thy surest hope is from the Church which false friends would have thee fear. Believe me, no hearts love thee more ardently than Catholic hearts, no tongues speak more honestly thy praises than Catholic tongues, and no hands will be lifted up stronger and more willing to defend, in war and in peace, thy laws and thy institutions than Catholic hands. *Esto perpetua.*[21]

In his lectures, Archbishop Ireland repeatedly expounds upon the American sense of destiny and mission and makes it his own.[22] It is especially interesting to see how—in the following passage—he intertwines the American mission and the Catholic mission, implying that the triumph of the former will allow the accomplishment of the latter:

. . . We cannot but believe that a singular mission is assigned to America, glorious for itself and beneficent to the whole race, the mission of bringing about a new social and political order, based more than any other upon the common brotherhood of man, and more than any other securing to the multitude of the people social happiness and equality of rights. With our hopes are bound up the hopes of the millions of the earth. The Church triumphing in America, Catholic truth will travel on the wings of American influence, and encircle the universe.[23]

At the time at which Ireland spoke, there was missing, of course, the sharp awareness, more common today among churchmen, that, in the long run, the spiritual mission does not benefit by conjunction with temporal imperialism. But it is evident that the possibility of conflict (or even divergence) between the two never entered into Archbishop Ireland's rather simplistic scheme of thought. In fact, he could proclaim

glibly: "In the eyes of the Church loyalty to country is loyalty
to God," without seeing any possibility that either this or its
converse might not be always true, and that loyalty to God
might in conscience exact from a man behavior which, in the
eyes of some of his fellow citizens, might appear to be dis-
loyalty. When the Archbishop proclaimed that "patriotism is
a heavenly virtue, a high and holy form of obedience," he
obviously did not envision that the Christian conception of a
law higher than that of man (to which the critics of the
one-hundred-percent Americanism appealed[24]) could place a
human being in a dilemma. Admittedly, in our own post-Nazi
era, it is easier for the Christian to see that there can be conflict between "the altar and the flag," and that (using John
Ireland's words) it does not automatically follow that "the
patriot dying for his country wears the halo of the martyr."
But Archbishop Ireland, on the defensive that his Americanism as a Catholic could be challenged, was not alert to such
distinctions. He could not agree that "in the last analysis . . .
when the altar and the flag are in conflict, the altar takes
precedence,"[25] because he could not (or did not) allow himself to conceive that such a conflict could exist. And so he
wrote:

. . . When I am asked: Do you put Church before Country, or
Country before Church? I reply: I neither put Church before
Country, nor Country before Church. Church and Country work
in altogether different spheres. My Church enjoins obedience to
itself in its own sphere, and obedience to Country within its sphere.
The Church is supreme in one order of things; the State is supreme
in another order . . .[26]

Apparently intent on demonstrating Catholic acceptance
of the American order of the separation of Church and State,
Ireland never wrote anything which indicated that he was
aware that, whether there is institutional separation or not,

there can still be the dilemma of nationalism. According to the definition used in this study, nationalism includes "the acceptance of the nation as the ultimate arbiter of human affairs." Was Archbishop Ireland willing thus to accept the nation as final arbiter? Is God the judge of the nation, or does the nation decide what is the judgment of God? This is the dilemma which, according to available evidence, Ireland never faced,[27] or whose theoretical possibilities he never pondered.[28]

It seems evident that Archbishop Ireland was too busy demonstrating how really American the Catholic Church is and attempting to integrate Catholicism into American life by showing how well it could serve the nation ("The undying religious spirit of the people is the surest hope of the Republic")[29] to consider the role of religion as transcending the nation and setting before the judgment of God the claims and the goals of the nation. Apparently he envisioned his task as an ecclesiastic as being the same as the work of Cardinal Gibbons, whose successful accomplishment he proclaimed on the occasion of Gibbons' silver jubilee as a bishop:

The work of Cardinal Gibbons forms an epoch in the history of the Church in America. He has made the Church known to the people of America; he has demonstrated the fitness of the Church for America,[30] the natural alliance existing between the Church and the freedom-giving democratic institutions of America . . . He, the great churchman, is also the great citizen. In him Church and country are united, and the magnetism of the union pervades the whole land, teaching laggard Catholics to love America, teaching well-disposed non-Catholics to trust the Church . . .[31]

## "THE AMERICAN OF AMERICANS"

On the occasion of the centenary celebration of the Constitution, held in Philadelphia in September, 1887, Cardinal Gibbons demonstrated in the happiest light to his non-Catholic fellow citizens the moving loyalty he felt as an American for the Republic which had given him birth. The love of Gibbons for his Church and its doctrines was beyond question; his love for his country and its institutions never showed to better advantage than when he saluted the century of the American Constitution and joined so wholeheartedly in its commemoration.[32]

"The American of Americans"—as Ireland had called him[33] —thus showed, as he had shown and was to show on numerous occasions, how accepted the Catholic Church had become, in his person, as truly *American*. Early in his career, this prince of the Church had written that "We should not let Protestants surpass us in our expression of loyalty and devotion to our country."[34] In July, 1879, he was already writing Cardinal Simeoni "of the good feeling which now subsists between the civil authorities and the Church."[35] Throughout his long ecclesiastical career, Cardinal Gibbons repeatedly set forth to the Holy See policies which he felt favored the continued acceptance of the Church as truly American. Thus, in his memorial to Simeoni urging that the Holy See refrain from condemnation of the Knights of Labor, the Cardinal educed, as a powerful argument against such condemnation, the risk "of having the Church regarded as un-American."[36] On another occasion he wrote Simeoni that "It is evident that everyone in our free America appreciates the important influence of the Catholic Church for the grandeur and prosperity of the nation . . ."[37] At the time of his accession to the cardinalate, he remarked on the harmony of American and Catholic institutions:

Our country has liberty without license, and authority without despotism. She rears no wall to exclude the stranger from among us. She has few frowning fortifications to repel the invader, for

she is at peace with all the world. She rests secure in the consciousness of her strength and her good will toward all. Her harbors are
open to welcome the honest emigrant who comes to advance his
temporal interests and find a peaceful home.

But, while we are acknowledged to have a free government,
perhaps we do not receive the credit that belongs to us for having,
also, a strong government. Yes, our nation is strong, and her
strength lies, under the over-ruling guidance of Providence, in the
majesty and supremacy of law, in the loyalty of her citizens and in
the affection of her people for her free institutions.[38]

Of this sermon, Cardinal Gibbons' biographer Will remarks:

Here was a Cardinal, barely out of his first consistory, daring to
assert in the very citadel of the Church that separation in the
United States did not mean hostility by the State to the Church,
but protection; that in the air of perfect freedom, unhampered by
political bonds, the Church could work out her Divine mission
better and more quickly . . .[39]

If at Rome and to Vatican officials Gibbons was at pains
to show how salutary American air was for the mission of the
Church, in season and out of season in the United States itself
he lost no opportunity of showing how well the Catholic
Church fit into American life and how well she harmonized
with American institutions. As has already been remarked,[40]
Will's biography reads like a panegyric to Gibbons as an
American citizen, but—as has already been noted—this was
the portrait of himself by which Gibbons wanted to be remembered. In Will's two-volume biography, in addition to the two
final chapters of eulogies and tributes to the Cardinal's Americanism, there are repeated references to his patriotism, to his
outstanding citizenship, to his efforts to show the congruence
of the Catholic Church with American institutions, and to

the acceptance by his fellow citizens of the Cardinal and his Church as being really American.[41] While the Ellis biography of the Cardinal attempts to correct what its author considered a one-sided portrait,[42] the final picture of Cardinal Gibbons and his efforts to show how American is the Catholic Church is not appreciably different.[43]

Of a gentler temper than Archbishop Ireland, Cardinal Gibbons' speeches and sermons and writings are not marked with the former's fierce patriotism or impassioned efforts to "make the Church throb with American life." The message conveyed, however, is the same. Like Archbishop Ireland, the Cardinal believed the Church must Americanize the immigrants and thus keep the American character of Catholicism above suspicion; like Archbishop Ireland, he urged on the immigrants complete identification with this land of destiny.[44] Like Archbishop Ireland, who was wont to take the Anglo-Saxon American virtues as the norm of the Catholic immigrants' conduct,[45] Cardinal Gibbons urged those who came to the United States to "be models of the natural virtues and practice thrift, perseverance, honesty, and fidelity to contracts, all of which Americans admired so much."[46]

Like Ireland, Gibbons was evidently quite unaware of any dilemma of nationalism for the Church. Alluding to a sight which he had witnessed in a parade held in his honor of the American flag and the Papal flag carried side by side, he said: "I always wish to see those two flags lovingly entwined, for no one can be faithful to God without being faithful to his country."[47] Will comments:

Above all, he was as firmly persuaded as a man could be of anything, that the Church's destiny here and the nation's destiny were one. The confusion of one would be the confusion of the other; the welfare and stability of one were the welfare and stability of the other.[48]

In his famous sermon in Milwaukee in August of 1891—
at the height of the Cahensly controversy—Cardinal Gibbons
developed the idea of

the double loyalty that should motivate American Catholics, love
of God and of country, and he exhorted his audience to glory in
the title of American citizen. There was but one country to which
American Catholics owed allegiance and that was the United
States, and it mattered not whether it was the land of their birth or
their adoption. Directing his remarks to the Catholic foreign-born,
the cardinal stated that when they decided to cross the Atlantic
to seek a new home in this country they should be animated by
the spirit of Ruth in the Old Testament when she determined to
join her kindred in the land of Israel. Gibbons would have the
Catholic immigrant say in the words of Ruth: "Whithersoever thou
shalt go, I will go: and where thou shalt dwelt, I also will dwell.
Thy people shall be my people, and thy God my God."[49]

Did this prince of the Church forget that *"thy* God" and
*"my* God" in the Christian dispensation are now the same?
The immigrants changed their nation, not their God. It seems
to the present writer that this Old Testament quotation (coming as it does from a period in which each nation was conceived of as having its own god) is especially inappropriate;
but Gibbons is not to be criticized on a problem of exegesis;
rather the whole sermon reveals his apparent inability to see
that the Catholic is not called upon simply to exchange one
nationalism for another, but rather to rise above accepting
the nation as "final arbiter of human affairs" in adhering to
God who transcends any particular nation.[50] Like Archbishop
Ireland, however, Cardinal Gibbons never examined the
"double loyalty" of which he spoke so eloquently and so frequently. For awareness of the possible dilemmas involved in
nationalism, we must turn to another member of the American
hierarchy, John Lancaster Spalding.

"THE POWER OF NATIONAL PREJUDICE . . ."

Bishop Spalding did not feel impelled, as did Cardinal Gibbons and Archbishop Ireland, to prove himself an "American of Americans." He differed from them in other ways as well. As has already been indicated he had much more tolerance for cultural diversity and reacted much less violently to the Cahensly episode. Besides, he was much less prone than Ireland and Gibbons to take American Protestant standards as the norm by which Catholicism and Catholics should be measured. Thus, for example, he did not feel himself to be on the defensive because Protestant countries could be shown to have greater material prosperity. ("Shall we say that the greed of gain which is so marked a feature in the populations of England and the United States is at once the result and proof of true Christian faith? May it not be barely possible that the value of material progress is exaggerated?"[51]) Neither was he ready to concur with Archbishop Ireland that *drink* was the worst evil and that the saloon was an un-American institution.[52]

But, in terms of this study, Bishop Spalding is of interest precisely because he apparently was well aware of the dangers of growing nationalism in the post-Civil War period and throughout his episcopate attempted to warn against it. In a volume published in 1877, he wrote:

The power of national prejudice is almost incredible. "Our country, right or wrong," is, we believe, an American phrase; but it expresses a sentiment which is almost universally held to be right and proper. In international disputes men nearly always take sides with their own country, without stopping to inquire into the merits of the quarrel, which, indeed, the strong feeling that at once masters them would prevent them from being able to do.[53]

In two addresses particularly, both delivered after the Span-ish-American War, does Bishop Spalding show himself acutely critical of unthinking nationalism. In the one, entitled "The Patriot," delivered February 22, 1899, he said:

There is a higher love than love of country,—the love of truth, the love of justice, the love of righteousness; and he alone is a patriot who is willing to suffer obloquy and the loss of money and friends, rather than betray the cause of truth, justice, and righteous-ness, for only by being faithful to this can he rightly serve his country. Moral causes govern the standing and the falling of states as of individuals; and conquering armies move forward in vain, in vain the fleeting fabric of trade is spread, if a moral taint within slowly moulder all. The national life is at fault if it be not in harmony with the eternal principles on which all human life rests. The greatest and the noblest men when they meet rise into regions where all merely national distinctions are forgotten and tran-scended. In studying the works of a philosopher, a poet, or a man of science, we give little heed to what country he was born and lived in, so eager are we to learn the truth and beauty he reveals,— the truth and beauty, which are of no country, which are wide and all-embracing as the universe.[54]

Noting that "patriotism as understood by the ancients is but a partial virtue. When it is most intense, it is most narrow and intolerant,"[55] Bishop Spalding contrasts this attitude with what he thinks should be the attitude of his hearers: "for us, nationality has ceased to be the limit of individual sympathy."[56] He goes on to note that many causes, "of which the Christian religion is the deepest and most far-reaching,"[57] have made for the wider view of modern men which transcends national boundaries, and in the modern age, science, technology and commercial interdependence should encourage the trend toward internationalism. Emphasizing that "there is a higher love than the love of country, that the citizen can serve his country rightly only when he holds himself in vital communion with the eternal principles on which human life rests, and by which it is nourished,"[58] Bishop Spalding notes that "Democracy itself is not an end, but a means."[59]

In the second address, delivered at the Anti-Imperial meeting, held in Chicago, April 30, 1899, Bishop Spalding showed himself especially critical of the doctrine of Manifest Destiny to which many Americans had succumbed.[60] Urging Americans to pay no heed to the siren call of imperialism, he said:

Therefore we will not believe that the gaining of a few naval battles over a weak and unprepared foe had power to throw us into such enthusiasm or such madness as to turn us permanently from the principles and policies to which we owe our national existence, our life and liberty; or that Destiny, the divinity of fatalists and materialists, can weaken our faith in the God of justice, righteousness and love, who scorns and thrusts far away those who, having the giant's strength, use it to oppress or destroy the weak and ignorant.

We have never looked upon ourselves as predestined to subdue the earth, to compel other nations, with sword and shell, to accept our rule; we have always believed in human rights, in freedom and opportunity, in education and religion, and we have invited all men to come to enjoy these blessings in this half a world which God has given us; but we have never dreamed that they were articles to be exported and thrust down unwilling throats at the point of the bayonet.[61]

Critical of the desire for material gain which he felt was behind American desire for expansion, Bishop Spalding spoke strongly:

We have money enough already, and our wealth is increasing rapidly. What we have to learn is how to live, how to distribute our money, how to take from it its mastery over us and make it our servant. Our capital is fast becoming the most inhuman, the most iniquitous tyrant the world has ever known. Its tyranny is a blight and curse to those who exercise it, as well as to the multitude who are its victims.[62]

He continued:

We are the victims of commercialism, we have caught the contagion of the insanity that the richest nations are the worthiest and most enduring. We have lost sight of the eternal principle that all freedom is enrooted in moral freedom, that riches are akin to fear and death, that by the soul only can a nation be great.[63]

Bishop Spalding ended his denunciation of imperialism with a plea to the American people:

. . . let them not stop to think what other nations will say, but let them, as becomes a great, a free, an enlightened people, be self-directed, holding in view only such aims and ends as are wise and just, and conducive to the permanent welfare and highest interest of the Republic.[64]

It is interesting to note that, while Archbishop Ireland and Cardinal Gibbons saw the cause of religion as bound up with the cause of democracy, Bishop Spalding was much more aware that the two had to be disentangled, that religion must sound the transcendent note, and that "Democracy itself is not an end, but a means." To Spalding, *eternal principles* not *Americanism* remained the norm of judgment, and he seemed especially wary of those who praised religion for its practical ends. While Ireland and Gibbons again and again were intent on demonstrating how useful religion is for good citizenship, and how religion remains the strong support of the nation,

Spalding showed himself highly critical of a religion cherished and espoused out of utility. He wrote:

Our religion and our education are cherished for the practical ends which they serve; for the support they give to our political institutions, while these institutions themselves are made a kind of fetish.[65]

Bishop Spalding's awareness of the dilemma of nationalism —that there could be a conflict between the demands of Caesar and God—is brought out in the following passage of an essay on Marcus Aurelius:

The ancients looked upon religion as essentially a national affair. They had no conception of what we understand by liberty of conscience. The appeal from Caesar to God was for them meaningless, if not impious. When the Christians declared that they were ready to obey all civil and military laws, but reserved to themselves freedom to worship God according to the principles of their faith, which forbade them to offer sacrifice to idols, they uttered words which their enemies could not understand, words which Christians themselves in later ages have often been unable or unwilling to understand.[66]

To understand the appeal from Caesar to God would imply an understanding that religion is *not* essentially a national affair and that, furthermore, religion does not exist to serve the nation. As Bishop Spalding noted, "A good patriot is first of all a good man,"[67] and a man who adheres to eternal principles will, in the long run, serve the nation well; but he is not a good man *in order to be* a good patriot. Urging people to be religious in order to be good citizens is perverting the order of means and ends, and turning what should be simply a desirable consequence into an intended result.[68]

More of an intellectual than Archbishop Ireland or Cardinal Gibbons, Bishop Spalding was more attuned to the danger of compromising the transcendental truth of religion by reducing it to a servant of the nation's purposes; besides, he evidently did not have the psychological need which they manifested to prove before non-Catholics how American they were as Catholics. (The two addresses of Spalding, highly critical of American nationalism, were delivered to non-Catholic audiences.)

However, the Spalding influence in the development of American Catholicism remained negligible, and it was the patriotic declamations of Cardinal Gibbons and Archbishop Ireland that at once set the pattern and the style for the hierarchical addresses in the years following.

### *"WHITE* FOR THE BASIC RIGHTEOUSNESS OF OUR NATIONAL PURPOSES"

Although one's first impression of the writings and addresses of Cardinal Spellman is that of remarkable similarity to those of Cardinal Gibbons and Archbishop Ireland, more careful study indicates an interesting difference. Both Cardinal Gibbons and Archbishop Ireland were out to prove to their hearers how American Catholicism really is; they never seemed to miss an opportunity—either on patriotic or religious occasions—to show the connection between religion and patriotism, and to acclaim the Catholic as the most loyal citizen. Cardinal Spellman, however, in his writings and addresses, seems to have accomplished the fusion of the themes of Catholicism and Americanism. No longer, as with Archbishop Ireland and Cardinal Gibbons, is there an attempt to connect the two themes; indeed, now they have become one. In a rather typical passage from his writings, in a selection called

"What America Means to Me," after speaking of America's material glories, the New York prelate says:

. . . but more precious and wondrous still is our Flag, which joyously and proudly I have seen flying aloft in all corners of the world, the flag of freedom that symbolizes justice and love of man for God and his fellowman, stark contradiction to the red flag of tyranny, symbol of serfdom and pagan oppression . . . *Red* with charity for all men and all nations of good-will—*Red* too with courage to achieve the liberties of men by personal sufferings and sacrifice; *White* for the basic righteousness of our national purpose; *Blue* for our trust and confidence in God, Our Heavenly Father, and, for those who are Catholic, *Blue* too with love for the Mother of God, to whom our forebears in the Faith long ago consecrated this land of loveliness, which, by the providence of Almighty God, is the last unfailing hope of embattled humanity struggling for survival against the menace of atheistic Communism that would desecrate and destroy both the flesh of man and man's spirit![69]

In this passage, the symbols of religion and of the nation are fused to such an extent that one has to re-read the selection to determine whether it is America or the Mother of God who is "the last unfailing hope of embattled humanity." In a prayer for America, whose initial line is, "Lord, lift this mighty host that is America,"[70] again a religious symbol is used to represent the national reality. The poem-prayer ends:

> We are a single host of grateful love for Thee,
> A single will for universal peace for men,
> A single soul of righteousness to come!
> Lord, lift this mighty host that is America,
> Reconsecrate us now in Thy Son's holy Name.
> Amen.

Again, a poem called "Magnificat of America"[71] combines America's mission and Mary's in the following lines:

America, Our America!
With dignity all sublime,
Thou art dedicated to Mary.
Her mission is through thee;
She feeds with thy hand;
She soothes with thy touch;
She frees with thy strength,
Giving homes through thee,
Spreading joy through thee,
To be light through thy light,
To be hope through thy hope,
To be love through thy love.

America's destiny and the essential righteousness of American national purposes are ever-recurring themes throughout Cardinal Spellman's published work. While the fusion of American and Catholic symbols is not always so evident as in the two poems quoted above, there is the repeated intertwining of religious and patriotic themes, the former frequently sanctioning the latter. Thus:

O God, Father of America:[72]
Thou has formed this Union of States, sealing it with high
    destiny,
That our nation be a light to all peoples in their dark
    despair, . . .[73]

The emphasis on America as a "single soul of righteousness" is evident. Even when, as in a Thanksgiving Day poem,[74] Cardinal Spellman supposedly exposes the sins of the nation to the judgment of God, the nation's goodness remains the dominant theme. Thus, following the lines:

Not as the Pharisee in righteous pride
But, rather, with the Publican we stand,
This blessed day, and render unto Thee
A double-motived thanks.

he thanks God for American virtues (like the publican?) and
for the fact that we have escaped the Communist threat. He
concludes:

> And these United States, united still
> In opposition, stand before the world,
> Above all passing pettiness and sloth,
> In one unflinching purpose—righteousness, . . .

It seems to the present writer that so closely does Cardinal
Spellman identify God and country, America and the Faith,
that it appears that he seems to do it spontaneously: it is no
longer an overt attempt—as it was in the days of Cardinal
Gibbons and Archbishop Ireland—to make and keep Catholicism acceptable to the American nation. Rather, it seems that,
in the fused symbols (and, indeed, in the reality) of nationalism and religion, Cardinal Spellman finds his own identity
and sense of solidarity with his fellows. "Leaders of a religion
will espouse nationalism not simply to keep their church
acceptable in the pluralist society, but out of the same need
for identity and the sense of belonging that motivates all
people in the given society."[75]

Evidence to support this insight is found in the circular
letters addressed by Cardinal Spellman to the priests and
faithful of the Archdiocese of New York. It could, perhaps,
be argued that the stress on the Americanism of Catholics and
Catholicism in Cardinal Spellman's published books is explic-
able on the basis that the Cardinal still feels under pressure to
prove to the country at large how American Catholicism really
is. However, the argument seems shaky on observing that he
would still feel it necessary to do this within the Catholic
community itself. And yet it is interesting to note that, in
letter after letter in which His Eminence appeals for the support of some charity or some Catholic institution, the reason

educed for the contributions of the faithful is a patriotic one. For instance, in a letter dated May 5, 1961, announcing the annual collection for St. Joseph's Seminary at Dunwoodie, the Cardinal writes:

> These newly ordained priests will join more than one thousand of their brother-priests laboring in many capacities in the 401 parishes of the Archdiocese, faithfully serving their fellowmen, inspiring and encouraging children and adults to become God-revering, home-loving, law-abiding patriotic citizens. Dedicated to carry on Christ's campaign of faith, justice and charity, zealously they work to counteract cold war campaigns of hate, bigotry and violence which are being fought fiercely and unceasingly by enemies of God, of America, and of free peoples everywhere.
>
> And, in the dread-filled days of bloodshed and misunderstanding, proudly and gratefully we remember our Chaplains, graduates too of our Seminary at Dunwoodie. Soldiers in the Army of Christ they bring God's Sacraments and your love to sons and daughters in America's Armed Forces encircling the globe.[76]

If we interpret the Cardinal's mind correctly, here is no apologetic defense of Catholicism as fitting in with the national purposes, here is no conscious effort in the face of the criticism of anti-Catholics to prove the utility of religion for the nation in producing loyal citizens; rather, the arguments for the support of religion based on national utility are the ones the Cardinal himself sees as relevant. The usefulness of Dunwoodie in producing chaplains and other priests who will make children and adults into "God-revering, home-loving, law-abiding citizens" is apparently uppermost in the Cardinal's own mind.[77]

In the same year, in a letter dated August 16, 1961, the Cardinal appeals for the school collection in the following words:

The perils and uncertainties facing all Americans these danger-ous days, make it vitally important for Catholic Americans to con-tinue faithfully and generously to help support our schools and their program of Catholic education.

Faithful Catholics make loyal citizens who prayerfully and grate-fully realize that one of the blessings of our great and glorious nation is the right of parents to educate their children according to their personal beliefs.[78]

In an appeal for The Catholic University, dated November 29, 1961, the Cardinal wrote:

Never in her history has America greater need for strong-minded, stout-hearted men and women of unshakeable faith and loyalty to help protect her and preserve her precious liberties from the enemies of God and freedom . . .

Only a country protected with the priceless endowment of a patriotic prayerful people can long endure and no nation is more powerful, no nation mightier than a country fortified by God-rever-ing, educated peoples.[79]

Again, in an appeal for the Bishops' Relief Fund, February 27, 1961, Cardinal Spellman gives evidence of the same need to associate the cause of religion with the American Way of Life. After detailing the accomplishments of this organization, he wrote:

Thus, this world-wide humanitarian organization has faithfully fulfilled its sacred obligation to God, to country and to man by practicing principles avowed in the humane documents which chartered our own charitable American way of life.[80]

In the following year, the Cardinal once more appealed to the Catholic faithful to respond to the needs to which the Bishops' Relief Fund ministers, urging that *"as God-loving Americans,* I know that you will again welcome the opportunity and privilege of generous helping."[81] (Emphasis supplied.)

One may ask why was not the appeal made to the faithful in their identity as Christians or Catholics? Is there evidence here that—leaving aside the primary identification which the lay Catholics of New York themselves may feel—the Cardinal himself feels comfortable in his primary identity as an American?[82]

In the light of Bishop Spalding's warning about revering religion for its practical usefulness for political institutions (which "themselves are made a kind of fetish"), one can consider this memorandum sent to all pastors of the New York Archdiocese, May 21, 1960, asking them to support Armed Forces Day. It stated:

As Americans we know that we cannot solely depend upon military strength . . . The inter-dependence of the deep and abiding religious faiths of Americans and our security may be recognized.[83]

The social utility of religion is thus recognized by religious men themselves, and Catholicism—no longer under the onus to prove its congruence with American life—is free to prove its usefulness by acting as a support to our military strength in assuring American security.

"Religion will be used to sanction the nationalist goals, to support them, and to encourage active adherence to them."[84]

*NOTES*

[1] Ireland, *The Church and Modern Society*, p. 151.

[2] In this post-Freudian era, it does not take any particular psychological astuteness to be able to point out that Ireland's use of the expres-

sion "the religion of patriotism," rather than "the religious duty of patriotism," cannot be dismissed simply as accidental theological sloppiness, but is, in reality, quite revealing of his own thoughts and sentiments of nationalism.

[3] *Loc. cit.*

[4] See Chapter 2, note 38.

[5] Guilday, *Life and Times of John Carroll,* p. 56, also p. 95.

[6] Melville, *John Carroll of Baltimore,* p. 103.

[7] *Ibid.*, p. 87, quoting Carroll's article in the *United States Gazette,* June 10, 1789.

[8] *Ibid.*, p. 103.

[9] *Ibid.*, p. 59. Guilday, *op. cit.*, p. 220.

[10] Carroll was well aware that the episcopacy was an institution viewed with horror by many of the colonists. Carl Bridenbaugh in *Mitre and Sceptre*: Transatlantic Faiths, Ideas, Personalities and Politics 1689–1775 (New York: Oxford University Press, 1962), p. xiii, notes that "the prediction that the arrival of bishops would mean violence was made seriously." In Chapter X, Bridenbaugh details the ferment that was aroused over rumors that Anglican bishops would be appointed in the colonies.

[11] Humphrey, *Nationalism and Religion in America* 1774–1789, p. 248.

[12] Browne, "Catholicism in the United States," in Smith and Jamison, *Religion in American Life,* Vol. I, p. 78.

[13] Guilday, *op. cit.*, p. 564.

[14] *Ibid.*, p. 392.

[15] *Loc. cit.*

[16] Ireland, *op. cit.*, p. 73.

[17] For Ireland, "The true Catholic must needs be the true patriot. In the eyes of the Church loyalty to country is loyalty to God; patriotism is a heavenly virtue, a high and holy form of obedience; the patriot dying for his country wears the halo of the martyr" (*ibid.*, p. 22).

[18] *Ibid.*, p. 180.

[19] See Chapter 2.

[20] Ireland, *op. cit.*, pp. 138–139.

[21] *Ibid.*, pp. 46–47.

[22] One wonders what the Canadians thought of Ireland's particular

sense of manifest destiny as revealed in the following statement made at the dinner of the Minnesota Society in New York, in December, 1902.

I do not want to be bellicose, but I say this for myself. As sure as fate, although you and I may not see it, the starry banner will wave mistress over all the territory from the gulf to the bay. There will be no conquest, no war. The hearts across the border are already beating with love for us, and commerce and agriculture are calling for espousals.—Moynihan, *The Life of Archbishop Ireland*, pp. 277–278.

Repeatedly, in speaking of the American mission, Ireland spelt out our destiny in terms of other peoples:

. . . There is not a country on the globe that does not borrow from us ideas and inspirations. The spirit of American liberty wafts its spell across sea and oceans, and prepares distant continents for the implanting of American ideas and institutions . . . —Ireland, *op. cit.*, p. 57.

The God-given mission of the Republic of America is not confined to its own people—it extends to all the peoples of the earth, to whom it is the symbol of human rights and of human liberty, and towards whom its flag flutters hope of future happiness.—*Ibid.*, p. 150.

In an address on "American Citizenship," Ireland showed himself to have assimilated well the Puritan concept of Americans as a chosen people with a mission in behalf of the rest of mankind:

. . . During all the long ages in which humanity was in travail with the precious liberties of democracy, the mighty God had been holding this land in reserve for the providential nation of the new times . . .

I have called America the providential nation. Even as I believe that God rules over men and nations, so do I believe that a divine mission has been assigned to the Republic of the United States. That mission is to prepare the world, by example and moral influence, for the universal reign of human liberty and human rights. America does not live for herself alone; the destinies of humanity are in her keeping.—*Ibid.*, pp. 173, 174.

[23] *Ibid.*, p. 58.

[24] See Curti, *The Roots of American Loyalty*, and Chapter 3.

[25] Curti, *ibid.*, p. 239.

[26] Ireland, *op. cit.*, p. 196.

[27] As will be seen in the next chapter, in the case of the Spanish-American War, which Ireland thought unjustified, it would seem that the dilemma was there but apparently Ireland was not aware of it as such.

[28] The confusion of the issue of the separation of Church and State (and the institutional prerogatives of each) with an entirely different question—the right and the obligation of the Church to witness to a

truth and a law higher than the claims of the nation—is met repeatedly in American Catholic history. Thus, as late as in a book published in 1932, Peter Guilday is explaining the silence of the Baltimore Councils prior to the Civil War on the slavery issue by pointing up the separation of Church and State and the "American distrust of ecclesiastical interference." He comments that the hierarchy "refused to break with the traditional policy of the Church which excluded rigorously all discussions of political debate. The prelates were face to face with problems of far greater moment than slavery in their efforts to keep abreast of the tide of immigration to our shores. No other Church in the land, then as now, has realized the supreme need of keeping itself free from political questions; and no other Church has sympathized more profoundly with the basic American distrust of ecclesiastical interference in public life." *A History of the Councils of Baltimore (1791–1884)* (New York: Macmillan, 1932), p. 182.

[29] Ireland, *op. cit.*, p. 178.

[30] Note how "America" is used as the norm.

[31] Ireland, *ibid.*, p. 110.

[32] Ellis, *The Life of James Cardinal Gibbons*, I, pp. 321–322.

[33] Ireland, *ibid.*, p. 111.

[34] Ellis, *ibid.*, I, p. 178.

[35] *Ibid.*, I, p. 193.

[36] *Ibid.*, I, p. 509.

[37] *Ibid.*, I, p. 251.

[38] Will, *Life of Cardinal Gibbons*, I, pp. 309–310. A slightly different version of this sermon is given in John Tracy Ellis, ed., *Documents of American Catholic History* (Milwaukee: Bruce, 1962), p. 459.

[39] Will, *ibid.*, p. 310.

[40] See Chapter 3.

[41] The present writer is faced with an over-profusion—over 180—of references to these matters which could be quoted.

[42] Ellis, *Life of Gibbons*, II, p. 659.

[43] Will's own nationalism seems to show through, however, especially in his exaggerated interpretation of the nationalities' controversy and Cahenslyism as "the greatest threat to the Catholic Church in America" (Will, *op. cit.*, I, p. 540). While Ellis cites Gibbons in a few passages (for instance, II, pp. 548, 560–561), as being critical of American society, he nowhere shows Gibbons as being aware of any of the

possible dilemmas of nationalism and his final evaluation of the Cardinal in II, Chapter XXIV, "American Citizen," leaves the Will's portrait virtually unmodified.

[44] Will, *ibid.*, pp. 404–406.

[45] See, for example, Ireland's stress on temperance.

Now in the convictions of the American people, and as a plain matter of fact, the American saloon is the personification of the vilest elements in our modern civilization . . . The Church that would prove herself to the country to be the Church of Christ must speak and act boldly against the saloon. —Ireland, *op. cit.*, p. 302.

[46] Ellis, *ibid.*, I, p. 383, paraphrasing Gibbons' article, "Irish Immigration to the United States."

[47] Will, *ibid.*, I, p. 390.

[48] *Ibid.*, I, p. 543.

[49] Ellis, *ibid.*, I, pp. 376–377.

[50] Will remarks (*op. cit.*, p. 507) that "one of the staunchest convictions to which he [Gibbons] adhered throughout his life was that homogeneity in America was a fundamental need in the absence of a repressive government which might maintain unity by force." One wonders if Gibbons ever thought of the diversity which is supposedly part of the American democratic ideal, and whether the stress on unity of all American Catholics in becoming homogeneous did not cause him to over-look the universality of Christians (a supra-national reality) which is a deeper kind of "likeness."

[51] *Essays and Reviews*, p. 116.

[52] *Opportunity and Other Essays*, p. 201.

[53] *Essays and Reviews*, p. 152.

[54] *Opportunity*, p. 193.

[55] *Ibid.*, p. 194.

[56] *Ibid.*, p. 195.

[57] *Loc. cit.*

[58] *Ibid.*, p. 197. One resists with difficulty the temptation to continue quoting from this address. Appealing continually to the eternal truths transcending the nation, Bishop Spalding notes (p. 198): "To no purpose is the country great, if the men are small." Evidently under the provocation of the one-hundred-percent Americanism which he was fighting, Spalding said (pp. 200–201): "A good patriot is first of all a good man,—true to himself and true to his relations to his fellowmen. If false to himself, he is false to all. . . . It will, indeed, be easy for

him to make his patriotism a theme for declamation, and easy, too, to throw suspicion on the loyalty of others; but if he is not a real man, it is not possible that he should be a real lover of his country."

In the collection of aphorisms, *Glimpses of Truth*, Bishop Spalding echoes some of the sentiments of this address. Thus, on page 62, he writes: "One is not better for belonging to a powerful family or nation; but he has greater opportunities." On p. 160, "All laudation partakes of self-laudation. We extol our country, our religion, our party; whatever, in a word, we identify with ourselves."

59 *Opportunity*, p. 199.

60 It is interesting to note that Bishop Spalding evidently saw the driving out of Spain from her colonies as just, but felt it would be wrong to annex the conquered islands and thus become an imperial power (*ibid.*, p. 208).

61 *Ibid.*, p. 215.

62 *Ibid.*, p. 219.

63 *Ibid.*, p. 221.

64 *Ibid.*, p. 228.

65 *Thoughts and Theories of Life and Education*, p. 33.

66 *Glimpses of Truth*, p. 246.

67 Above, footnote 58.

68 In this connection one is reminded of a remark made by Schneider and Dornbusch (*Popular Religion*, p. 70) when they noted the emphasis in inspirational books on religion as a means to psychological adjustment: "When the religious begin to look on their own activity more or less in the manner of functionally oriented sociologists . . . with an eye to turning what are regarded as desirable consequences into desired results—it becomes a neat question whether they do not endanger the results they hope for."

69 *What America Means to Me*, p. 4.

70 *Prayers and Poems*, p. 3.

71 *What America Means to Me*, p. 15. It is rather odd that this poem takes the form of a prayer addressed to America, not to Mary or to God.

72 The mention in this poem of God as "Father of America" is not unique for Cardinal Spellman. Even in his poems that have supposedly an international theme, it is God as the God of America who dominates. Thus in a "Prayer for the United Nations," while the Cardinal

begins, "Father in Heaven, God of all nations," it is to mention of God's special relationship with America that he swiftly turns.

> America is Thine, O God of Nations,
> Thine to use for all nations' sake,
> Thine the breath o'er hill and valley
> And from sea to shining sea.
>
> . . . . . . . . . . . . . . . . . . . . . . . . . . . . . . . . . . . .
>
> Here within the council chambers of the nations,
> We pray that Thy Spirit of Peace may dwell,
> Nurtured by America's love for humanity,
> Served by America's passion for justice,
> Guarded by America's might and genius.
> —*What America Means to Me*, pp. 74–75.

That any other nation may have a contribution to make to this God-given mission is never suggested. One interprets the reference to "Thy Spirit of Peace" as to the Holy Spirit, were it not that He hardly needs to be "nurtured by America's love."

[73] "Prayer for America," *What America Means to Me*, p. 28.

[74] "Forever Thine," *ibid*., p. 23.

[75] This is one of the tentative hypotheses of the relationship between religion and nationalism in a pluralist society which will be discussed in Chapter 8.

[76] Archives of the New York Archdiocese.

[77] This is not to say that Archbishop Ireland and Cardinal Gibbons before him were not spontaneously patriotic too, but they spoke primarily out of an apologetic need, and not because the idea of Americanism was their habitual frame of mind which gave them their own identity.

[78] Archives of New York Archdiocese.

[79] *Ibid.*

[80] *Ibid.*

[81] *Ibid.*, letter dated April 23, 1962.

[82] See the incident recounted by Will Herberg, Chapter 1.

[83] Archives of the New York Archdiocese.

[84] Hypothesis to be discussed in Chapter 8.

# 6/First in War

*"Our hands are always lifted to bless her banners and her soldiers."*[1]

*"It is good for a people that supreme emergencies arise to test its patriotism to the highest pitch. If patriotism remains dormant for a long period it loses its strength, whereas the reflection and self-consciousness which resolute action awakens result in a fuller appreciation of the value of the country and the institutions which it is the duty of patriotism to defend."*[2]

These words of Archbishop Ireland seem to epitomize the attitude of the Catholic hierarchy, for the most part, to America's wars. As Henry J. Browne has remarked: "Certainly the tradition of patriotism in wartime—notwithstanding in recent times a growing fringe of conscientious objectors—has been a hallmark of the American Catholic community."[3] This active and enthusiastic support given to the nation's wars "has remained one of the most frequently used, if not logical, retorts to answer any aspersions on Catholic loyalty to American principles."[4]

John Gilmary Shea is considered responsible for the interpretation that, so great was the patriotism of Catholic Americans right from the beginning, that there were no Catholic Tories in the colonies during the Revolution. In an address before the United States Catholic Historical Society in 1884, Shea said:

The Catholics spontaneously, universally, and energetically gave their adhesion to the cause of America, and, when the time came, to American Independence. There was no faltering, no division, every Catholic in the land was a Whig. In the list of Tories and Loyalists, in the volumes written since about them, you cannot find the name of a single Catholic. There were no Catholic Tories.[5]

Guilday, however, educes evidence to show that Shea's estimation of Catholic participation was greatly exaggerated, and Browne expresses the considered opinion of historians today when he writes, "in general, Catholic support of the Revolution was as good as other segments of the population."[6]

John Carroll, in a letter to the *Columbian Magazine* in September, 1787, replied to an attack on the Catholics of the United States by pointing out that, even while the State of New Jersey was excluding them from the benefits of full citizenship, Roman Catholics were protecting her:

At that very time the American army swarmed with Roman Catholic soldiers, and the world would have held them justified, had they withdrawn themselves from the defence of a State which treated them with so much cruelty and injustice, and which they then covered from the depredations of the British army. But their patriotism was too disinterested to hearken to the first impulse of even just resentment.[7]

Although he used the phrase "the American army swarmed with Roman Catholic soldiers," Archbishop Carroll was usually more temperate in his language. Thus, in the article in the *United States Gazette* of June 10, 1789, he reiterated that the blood of Catholics, "in proportion to their numbers," had flowed as freely as that of any of their fellow citizens in the war for independence.[8]

During the events preceding the War of 1812, there seems to be evidence that Archbishop Carroll did not share the antipathy toward the British government that obsessed some of his fellow Americans. On January 27, 1812, he wrote his English friend Father Plowden: "Our American cabinet and a majority of Congress seem to be infatuated with a blind predilection for France and an unconquerable hostility to England."[9] Yet, Melville writes that, "Although the archbishop may have deprecated some of the policies which had led his nation into war, once that war was declared he put the full force of his influence on the side of the government."[10] In a sermon delivered August 20, 1812, he admonished his flock that theirs was a just war and that they must all contribute to the preservation of the nation.

We have witnessed the unremitting endeavours of our chief magistrate to continue to us the blessings of peace; that he has allowed no sentiments of ambition or revenge, no ardor for retaliation . . . to withhold him from bearing in his hands the olive branch of peace; We have seen him . . . renewing overtures of perfect friendship and cordial union, after his first proposals were contumeliously rejected. The ministers of peace, commissioned by him . . . left no means untried to effect his salutary and benevolent purposes.[11]

Baltimore's archbishop concluded his discourse with the reminder from St. Paul's Epistle to the Ephesians that "our wrestling is against principalities and powers, against the rulers of the world of darkness." His biographer comments: "If in the deepest recesses of his heart John Carroll believed that Napoleon and his forces were the more impious of the European forces in the struggle, he would keep these convictions buried."[12] Publicly, he did what his successors in the American hierarchy would do in each succeeding war: give unqualified support to the national cause and encourage full Catholic participation in the war.[13]

## "MORE WELCOME AS SOLDIERS"

About Catholic participation in the next in the sequence of America's wars, Browne makes the following trenchant comment:

If this period [of the Mexican War] marked the beginning of Catholic determination to prove they belonged on the American scene by bragging about the military achievements of their co-religionists, it may be remembered that they noticed how much more welcomed they were as soldiers than civilians.[14]

Guilday gives us the information that there were 1,100 Catholics in the Mexican War, and that "Father Rey [a chaplain] was killed after the capture of Monterey under General Scott, who, it was reported, wept when informed of his untimely fate."[15] Who was the source of this report which, on the surface at least, sounds like an embroidered legend? Guilday does not say.

Archbishop Hughes used the Mexican War to point up the loyalty of Catholics. In a lecture entitled "The Present Condition and Prospects of the Catholic Church in the United States," delivered January 17, 1856, he said:

If any say you are disloyal to the country, point to every battle from the commencement of the country, and see if Catholics were not equal in the struggle, and as zealous to maintain the dignity and triumph of the country as those with whom they fought! Nor was it in the contest with Great Britain alone, against whom it was supposed we have an hereditary spite, but against Catholic Mexico they fought with equal courage. Although they aimed the point of the sword at the breast of their brother Catholics, they aimed it not the less, and in every contest they endeavored to maintain liberty as well as right.[16]

The Mexican War was to prove only the first war in which American Catholics "aimed the point of the sword at the breast of their brother Catholics." The same thing, occurring at the time of the Spanish-American War, was used in similar fashion to prove the exceptional devotion to the nation of American Catholics. It is probably not without significance that later commentators seemed to react as did Archbishop Hughes and to see in this circumstance not a tragic dilemma or a sad irony of the human condition, but simply an example of Catholic patriotism about which they could justly brag.[17]

In the period between the Mexican War and the outbreak of the Civil War—if we are to believe Guilday—the American Catholic hierarchy remained aloof from the great issues that were tearing at the vitals of the nation. Describing the events of the First Plenary Council of Baltimore, convened in 1852, Guilday writes:

It seemed inevitable that, with the whole nation aroused to intense feeling, even as early as 1852, over the problem of slavery, Catholics and non-Catholics would expect the Council—the first of its kind in history—to cast its voice either with slavery or with abolition . . . When, therefore, as the Council proceeded, it became evident that the attending prelates had decided to keep silent on the question, neither condemning nor condoning slavery, Catholics realized more acutely than ever the real meaning of the Church's place in American life, and non-Catholics appreciated the fact that here was a body of American spiritual leaders who meant to bring to the disturbed condition of the times the one asset the country needed: peace and calm. Silence was the only boon which would quiet the dissension and would permit the problem to be solved naturally.[18]

Whether or not we dismiss this interesting *post factum* interpretation of the Council's silence on slavery as simply Guilday's own variety of triumphalism, it seems patently true that "silence" did *not* "quiet the dissension" and "the problem" was *not* "solved naturally." Indeed, the Civil War had erupted within the decade, and Catholics—prelates and people alike —were taking the side and supporting the stand of the region of the country in which they found themselves.

"THERE IS BUT ONE RULE FOR A CATHOLIC, WHEREVER HE IS"

In a letter to a southern bishop, Archbishop Hughes wrote:

. . . the flag on the cathedral [St. Patrick's in New York] was erected with my permission and approval. It was at the same time an act of expediency going before a necessity likely to be urged upon me by the dictation of enthusiasm in this city. I preferred that no such necessity of dictation should overtake us, because, if it had, the press would have sounded the report that Catholics were disloyal, and no act of ours afterward would successfully vindicate us from the imputation. On the whole, however, I think, my dear Bishop, that the Catholics of the North have behaved themselves with great prudence, moderation, and a dignity which had, for the moment at least, inspired, among the high and the low, great respect for them as a religious body in the Union. I regret that I cannot say as much for the Catholics and for some of the clergy in the South. In their periodicals in New Orleans, and in Charleston, they have justified the attitude taken by the South on principles of Catholic theology, which I think was an

unnecessary, inexpedient, and, for that matter, a doubtful if not a
dangerous position, at the commencement of so unnatural and so
lamentable a struggle.[19]

And yet, even though in the letter quoted above, Archbishop Hughes implied that he thought the southern Catholics
had gone too far in justifying the southern cause, he evidently
took for granted that it was right and proper for them to
support the cause itself. Thus, in a lecture delivered on St.
Patrick's Day, 1861, he said:

And in our own country, where there has been lately so much
excitement (all of which I trust, will terminate amicably), they
divide it into two parts, calling them North and South, and they
talk of division and civil war. Well, there is but one rule for a
Catholic wherever he is, and that is, to do his duty there as
citizen.[20]

Requested by the government to undertake a special mission
to England and France to plead the Union cause, Archbishop
Hughes thus explained his task in a letter to Cardinal Barnabo
of Propaganda:

The Government at Washington were pleased to think that, in
requesting me to accept this mission, they were paying a great
compliment to the whole Catholic people of the United States; and
they wished to give me also a mark of their confidence which
might go far, as an example for future administrations to be well
disposed toward the Catholics, and by this act to condemn that
spurious faction who, but a few years ago, under the name of
Know-Nothings, attempted to treat the Catholics of America as
disloyal citizens, unworthy of the equal privileges which the laws
of the country extend to all its inhabitants.[21]

Important as Archbishop Hughes evidently felt the Civil
War was as an opportunity for Catholics to prove their loyalty,

he nevertheless had earlier, October of 1861, expressed himself rather strongly in a letter to Mr. Cameron, Secretary of War:

There is being insinuated in this part of the country an idea to the effect that the purpose of this war is the abolition of slavery in the South. If that idea should prevail among a certain class, it would make the business of recruiting slack indeed. The Catholics, so far as I know, whether of native or foreign birth, are willing to fight to the death for the support of the constitution, the Government and the laws of the country. But if it should be understood that, with or without knowing it, they are to fight for the abolition of slavery, then, indeed they will turn away in disgust from the discharge of what would otherwise be a patriotic duty.[22]

However, Archbishop Hughes, who had succeeded in quieting the draft rioters in New York, was recognized as the exponent of Catholic loyalty. He urged military conscription and apparently did all that he could to support the war effort. In a brief biography published immediately after his death in 1864, the anonymous author wrote: "A better and more patriotic American than he never lived."[23]

In general, as Browne has noted, the Civil War was a great opportunity for American Catholics.[24] It was an opportunity to prove their loyalty and to grow in identity with the national purpose, as well as to increase their sense of solidarity with the country. As one enthusiastic recounter of Catholic participation in the Civil War put it, at the outbreak of war: "Immediately no voices were louder or more sincere than the Catholics in swelling the grand chorus that proclaimed: 'The Union must and shall be preserved.' "[25] "From hundreds of pulpits patriotic pastors exhorted their people to stand by the Union and support the President and his government."[26] The 69th Regiment had twice its quota ready to start for the front on April 23, 1861,[27] and, according to Meehan, regiments

almost wholly composed of Catholics volunteered from the
centres of crowded population.[28]

In March, 1862, Father Ireland, the future Archbishop of
St. Paul, received his commission as a chaplain. His biographer
describes him during the battle of Corinth:

. . . when the cry was raised that the ammunition was failing, he
was seen hurrying down the line, heedless of the bullets flying
round him, carrying a supply of ammunition and crying: "Here
are your cartridges, boys, don't spare them."[29]

Shea claims that Ireland as a chaplain "was not, however,
content with preaching. At times he went into battle and
fought with the men."[30]

Later on in life, Ireland was to hark back to Civil War
incidents.

In his address in the Milwaukee Auditorium on August 11,
1913, he thrilled his large audience by recounting an incident of
the battle of Gettysburg, when, at a crucial moment, Father William Corby, leaping to the top of a large boulder, cried out: "The
Catholic Church refuses Christian burial to the soldier who turns
his back to the foe or deserts his flag."[31]

Evidently for the rest of his days, Ireland enjoyed recalling
his own Civil War role. Abbé Felix Klein thus describes him
at a meeting of veterans in Washington, October 14, 1907,
on the occasion of the dedication of a monument to General
Sherman:

Once more the Archbishop became again the old chaplain of
the Fifth Minnesota Volunteers. Former companions in arms
thronged around him, and they dwelt on reminiscences of which I
knew nothing. The Army of the Potomac, whose reception we
were attending, resolved for this night to form a junction with the

Army of the Tennessee, which was bivouacked at another hotel. So, about half-past nine, to the strains of martial music, off we set, marching two by two, as solemnly as you please. Archbishop Ireland and an old officer headed the line, setting the step for us and looking positively war-like. The Archbishop, in fine spirits and full of vivacity, proudly wore his military medal.[32]

## "THE SACRED STIGMATA OF PATRIOTISM"

Archbishop Ireland himself said of the Civil War that it

. . . was the one test needed to give the Republic the full consciousness of her power, and never was she so strong in the elements of life, never so entrancing in beauty, never so menacing to the foes of democracy, as when the sun of Appomatox shone on her banner and revealed upon its azure ground the full galaxy of her stars.[33]

In his discourse on patriotism, delivered April 4, 1894, Archbishop Ireland, addressing an audience of whom "Many . . . carry on breast and face the sacred stigmata of patriotism,"[34] spoke of the duties of citizenship in peace and war.[35] When the speech was published, the following was added as a cautionary footnote:

No doubt, war waged in defense of the life or other supreme interest of country intensifies the patriotism of a people. War, however, is not to be brought on for the mere purpose of intensifying patriotism . . . War is dreadful; but there are things yet more dreadful . . . The movement toward settling of all controversies through arbitration is most praiseworthy . . . But will nations so advance in Christian civilization that, in fact, pride and passion will everywhere yield to the command of reason, and that the sacred rights of men and nations will need no other protection than the voice of a tribunal of justice? . . . this ideal condition . . . is somewhat remote from the present time; and, meanwhile, the safety of a nation lies in readiness to give battle for its own vital interests or those of humanity.[36]

Concerning Archbishop Ireland's attitude toward the Spanish-American War, his biographer writes:

Although his sympathies in the days preceding the declaration of war against Spain were largely with that unfortunate country, which, he felt, was drawn into an unnecessary conflict against the wishes of the President, nevertheless, once war was declared, he gave wholehearted support to the government, and he gloried in the manifestation of unity among the people, of thousands animated with one ambition—service to their country.[37]

Evidently, neither Ireland nor his biographer were bothered by the fact that the war was "an unnecessary conflict":

He (Ireland) gave little consolation to pacifists. On October 17, 1898, in company with President McKinley and ex-President Harrison, he spoke in the Auditorium in Chicago, at a benefit for suffering soldiers and sailors. Beginning with an apostrophe to peace and a picture of the horrors of war he insisted that there are times when war is necessary, that more horrible than war is the destruction of social security, the disruption of the nation, its enslavement to foreign power, the robbery of its territory, or the possible lowering of its flag through disgrace abetted by cowardice.
Archbishop Ireland was a patriot both in theory and in practice . . . Again, in 1908 when the country was in danger from pacifists, who were making their influence felt among the people, he stood before the House committee and begged for preparedness in words which have a message for our time:[38] "I have always believed that the best way to have peace is to be ready for war. A good deal is said nowadays against the army and against the spirit of war. The idea of universal peace is very good, but to make it a gospel is a mistake."[39]

## "THE DUTY OF THE HOUR IS WARLIKE ARDOR"[40]

Shea claimed that over half of those lost on the battleship *Maine* were Catholics:[41] Writing at the time of the Spanish-American War, he said that nearly half the enlisted men in the Navy prior to and during the War were Catholics.[42] Elsewhere he noted that, while Catholics of the time made up one-seventh of the population of the United States, they constituted between one-fourth and one-third of the men in the Army and Navy.[43] On the basis of these facts, he made the following comment:

When we reflect that this war was one waged against a Catholic country . . . surely our non-Catholic brethren will not allow prejudice to prevent them from rising to a full appreciation of how grandly their Catholic fellow citizens have again given conclusive evidence that our country can always rely upon them . . .[44]

Shea refers to a sermon preached by Archbishop Ireland (whom he calls "that typical American") at the end of the Spanish-American War in which the prelate said:

Why has God given us victory and greatness? It is not that we take pride in our power . . . It is that Almighty God has assigned to this republic the mission of putting before the world the ideal of popular liberty, the ideal of the high elevation of all humanity.[45]

In response to President McKinley's request that the nation express its thanks for the triumph of American arms, Cardinal Gibbons prepared a letter which was read in all the churches of the Archdiocese of Baltimore on Sunday, July 17, 1898. In that letter he asked Catholics to give thanks to God for the victories and to pray for the souls of those who had died in the fighting.[46]

Given the difference in temperament, Cardinal Gibbons' attitude in the months preceding the Spanish-American War, and during the War itself, greatly resembled that of Archbishop Ireland. When on February 28, 1898, a requiem Mass had been offered for the victims of the *Maine,* the Cardinal "first paid tribute to patriotism as a virtue, and remarked that we did not realize how much we loved our country until a crisis was upon it."[47] However, Ellis regards as the most important part of the sermon Gibbons' words on the forbearance that all Americans should exercise:

This nation is too brave, too strong, too powerful, and too just to engage in an unrighteous or precipitate war. Let us remember the eyes of the world are upon us, whose judgment we cannot despise, and that we will gain more applause and credit for ourselves by calm deliberation and masterly inactivity than by recourse to arms.[48]

But forbearance was not exercised, and even though Spain capitulated to the American terms on April 9, Congress passed, on April 19, a four-point resolution which was tantamount to a declaration of war. Six days later, war was formally declared. The *Washington Post* of May 4, 1898 quotes a statement of Cardinal Gibbons to the effect that:

Catholics in the United States have but one sentiment. Whatever may have been their opinions as to the expediency of the war, now that it is on they are united in upholding the government.[49]

Ellis comments:

The judgment of posterity has long since been established that if the counsels of Gibbons and those who shared his views in the early days of 1898 had been followed, the United States might have been spared the ignominy of provoking an unjust war. But once war was declared the cardinal's conduct left nothing to be desired from the point of view of a loyal citizen.[50]

In other words, the Cardinal supported the war, even though he felt it was unjustified. Nothing his biographers tell us gives us grounds to think that he experienced any conscientious dilemma in following this course of action. For him and for Archbishop Ireland (as for Ellis who clearly brands the war as unjust), there was no other course to follow. Tacitly at least, they had accepted the nation as the final arbiter of human affairs.

### "OUR PEOPLE WILL RISE AS ONE MAN"

We believe that our country's heroes were the instruments of the God of Nations in establishing this home of freedom; to both the Almighty and to His instruments in the work, we look with grateful reverence; and to maintain the inheritance of freedom which they have left us, should it ever—which God forbid—be imperilled, our Catholic citizens will be found to stand forward, as one man ready to pledge anew "their lives, their fortunes, and their sacred honor."[51]

In the first World War, as previously in the Spanish-American War, the Catholics of the nation redeemed that pledge. According to Will, under the leadership of Gibbons the Catholics were the first religious body to pledge their support.[52] On April 18, 1917, twelve days after Congress had declared war, the archbishops, at their annual meeting, adopted a resolution affirming that "Our people, as ever, will rise as one man to serve the nation."

Moved to the very depths of our hearts by the stirring appeal of the President of the United States, and by the action of our National Congress, we accept whole-heartedly and unreservedly the decree of that legislative authority proclaiming this country to be in a state of war.[53]

Upon declaration of war, Cardinal Gibbons issued this statement to the press:

The primary duty of a citizen is loyalty to country. This loyalty is manifested more by acts than by words; by solemn service rather than by empty declaration. It is exhibited by an absolute and unreserved obedience to his country's call. . . . The members of both Houses of Congress are the instruments of God in guiding us in our civic duties . . .[54]

Made honorary chairman of a group called the League of National Unity, organized in October, 1917, the Cardinal wrote President Wilson that "We are working to the end that our countrymen may see the folly and grave disobedience of unjust and ill-tempered criticism of national policies."[55] On Sunday, October, 18, which the President had declared a day of prayer for the success of American arms, Cardinal Gibbons "took the opportunity to insist upon the paramount duty of obedience on the part of citizens to their government," and he cautioned against criticizing its policies in wartime.[56]

"He knew and loved the Church and the American Republic with an intensity that was excelled by no American of his age," says Ellis of Gibbons.[57] It is apparent that in his active patriotism during the World War he was very much aware that the Catholic Church still had to prove her Americanism to some of the nation's citizens. Thus, when Archbishop Ireland wrote him, "It is delightful to notice how you are holding the Church in the foreground in these meaningful days of war," the Cardinal replied:

I am trying to do all that I can that the Church may be of full service to the country during these trying days, and that no ground will be left after the ordeal is over upon which the enemies of the Church might endeavor to raise up unfair charges against her.[58]

The day before the Armistice was signed, Cardinal Gibbons preached to the soldiers at Camp Meade, Maryland:

We have conquered because we believe that righteousness exalteth a nation . . . We have conquered because we have fought for the eternal principles of truth and because we realize that our hope and our independence, our trust and our success, repose in Him who is alike the God of battles and of justice.[59]

## "AMERICA HAS BEEN INVARIABLY VICTORIOUS"

When the combatants put down their arms after World War I, historians took up the pen to expose the origins of the sanguinary struggle, and many causes of the war were listed in books that have been published in the last two decades. By these authors the World War was explained in its beginnings by the rivalry of nations for power and wealth, their quest for territorial expansion and imperial domination, their seeking of new markets and outlets for capital investment, their attempt to take advantage of backward people, motives, all of them, materialistic, sordid and ignoble.

If these were the underlying causes of World War I, American soldiers knew nothing of them. These were not the motives that stirred their minds and inspired them with the will for victory. Theirs was an unselfish crusade. They fought for pure and high ideals.[60]

In a book published shortly after the United States entered the World War II, (the then Archbishop) Spellman attempted to explain the origin of the war:

Despite the failure in the realization of our aims in World War I we still remain idealists. To be otherwise is impossible for Americans. But experience has taught us a measure of realism . . . We know now that we cannot continue to remain unarmed when other countries have not imitated our peaceful example. We know now that it is our pressing duty to defend ourselves, our lives, our liberties, and our institutions . . .[61] . . . and although we have envied none, have wronged none and have coveted nothing, although we have shared our abundance with a distressful world and have felt ourselves charged to do so before God and men, our good will has not been reciprocated.[62]

Clearly New York's archbishop identified the American cause in the war with the cause of the Church:

Our President and our Holy Father have combined the forces of our great country, and the forces of religion in a battle for peace . . .

We can do our part to further the program of peace to strengthen the forces of the nation and the Church in their moral battles for peace . . .[63]

The cause of America for Spellman is a cause whose intrinsic justice even enemy peoples must recognize:

Our free press and free radio bring us the words of the leaders of the powers of darkness ranged against us, ofttimes false and sometimes ridiculous. The oppressed, suffering, deluded and eventually rebellious, defeated people of the nations ranged against us know nothing of the attitude of the United States except that they must know in their hearts that America is on the level and on the square. Their leaders cannot squelch that thought nor can they suppress the knowledge that America has been invariably victorious. And she will be victorious again, cost what it may.[64]

But not only for Cardinal Spellman was America in World War II "on the level and on the square," but her suffering and dying soldiers could be compared to Christ:

Then a Man suffered and died to save His fellow man, to bring peace to the hearts of all men. His mission was one of Divine mercy; His objective, every soul; His weapon, love; His way, the Commandments.

These young American airmen with whom I was living, wanted to believe and did believe that they too were suffering and dying to bring salvation and peace to their fellow men . . .[65]

And he concludes his poem, *The Risen Soldier*:

> I am the risen soldier; though I die
> I shall live on and, living, still achieve
> My country's mission . . .
> . . . . . . . . . . . . . . . . . . . . . . . . . . . . . . .
> . . . . . .And if it be
> My blood should mingle reverently with Christ's,
> His Son's, in this my final missioning,
> Shall I not whisper with my dying breath—
> "Lord, it is sweet to die—as it were good
> To live, to strive—for these United States,
> Which, in Your wisdom, You have willed should be
> A beacon to the world, a living shrine
> Of Liberty and Charity and Peace."[66]

Christ, the Risen Soldier, is the American dying for his country. The symbols of the nation and the symbols of religion have become one. In Cardinal Spellman's novel, *The Foundling*, the hero describes a sermon given by the Catholic chaplain on December 8, 1941: "He told us that America has been dedicated to Our Blessed Mother, and that if our country was being forced to declare war on her feast day, Mary would see us through."[67]

At the end of the war, the Cardinal wrote "A Prayer of Thanksgiving After Victory":

> O God of Destiny!
> Our nation, still bleeding from the wounds of war,
> Thanks Thee for the Victory of this Hour,
> Won by our valiant dead,
> Our soldiers' blood,
> Our country's tears.
> We were not alone when we groped through the night of war,
> When we drank the cup of grief,
> Thou, Lord God of Hosts, wert with us,
> For we were with Thee.[68]

God's cause and our cause were one. Cardinal Spellman saw the United States as having fought from a motive of charity:

> If ever it were possible for a nation to fight out of a motive of charity to neighbor as well as for its own life, that possibility and the actuality are ours today. If ever we have looked for a deeper meaning for the stars and stripes of our flag, the white of justice and the red of charity, we know we have found it today. Every moment, every drop of blood and of sweat, every hour of fatiguing labor, every wound of our poor, torn humanity can and must be consecrated today to the defense of our country and the cause of charity, which is ultimately God's cause.[69]

It is interesting to note that, even though America's ally in World War II was Communist Russia (a fact which did bother some American Catholics and was later to bother Cardinal Spellman himself and lead to his break with President Roosevelt), the Archbishop of New York apparently never saw the issues at stake in other than black-and-white terms. His quotation of a soldier's words could reflect his own attitude: "Life is not complex; I have a God to serve, a soul to save, a family and country to love, to live and die for."[70] For Cardinal Spellman there does not seem ever to have been a dilemma, especially in wartime.

> Our foes are Thy foes,
> They plot to destroy Thee;
> They fight to fetter us,[71]

thus completely simplified did the issue become in the Korean War. For then our enemies were the Communists who were, for Cardinal Spellman, quite unambiguously identical with the powers of darkness.[72]

O Lord of Hosts, bless and protect the legions of our armed forces in their crusade to defend and vindicate the ideals of human freedom; bless them and the thousands of martyrs who have been called to lay down their lives on the rugged mountainsides and in the rice-paddies of Korea . . .[73]

In the eyes of Cardinal Spellman, the American soldiers "defending the American way of life," were fighting in Korea for the freedom "to adore the true God by day and by night."[74]

> Our rights are ours by right Divine and Eternal,
> To have and to hold against all aggression . . .[75]

## RIGHT TO SAY *NO* TO THE NATION?

Let us pray that the world may never again see such a disgraceful day as that of Hiroshima, that men may never again place their trust, their calculations and their prestige in such nefarious and dishonorable weapons.

Thus spoke Pope Paul VI on the twentieth anniversary of Hiroshima, solemn words commemorating the bombing which had ushered in the era of nuclear warfare. At the least, these words imply a criticism of the United States for the explosion of the first atomic bomb on a civilian population; yet Cardinal Spellman, like the vast majority of the Catholic hierarchy of the United States, has remained silent, never voicing any criticism at all of the way America achieved the end of the war against Japan.

But the issue of nuclear warfare inevitably is with us, and discussion at the Second Vatican Council, on the position of the Church in the modern world, inevitably touched on the question of the morality of nuclear weapons. While Cardinal Spellman kept silence on the particular issue of nuclear weapons, he did speak out in the fourth session of Vatican II, when Schema 13 was discussed by the Council Fathers.[76] Speaking against the section of Schema 13 which re-affirmed the right to conscientious objection, the Cardinal is reported by United Press International as saying: "Military service certainly can be made obligatory, and it should be made clear that individuals cannot refuse to do this service." According to Religious News Services, the Cardinal added, "In such cases the individual cannot arrogate to himself the right to accept or to refuse obedience." The NC report noted that the Cardinal "said clarification [in Schema 13] is needed to state that military service is obligatory."[77]

The Cardinal's statement seems especially surprising as it followed, by only a week, his previous intervention on behalf of the decree on religious liberty. On the earlier occasion the Cardinal had defended the individual's right of conscience to worship God. If he urged (as he did) that the individual should be free from the coercion of the Church in the matter of religious worship, even though his conscience is objectively erroneous, one could expect that he would respect the same

right of conscience for the individual in the matter of warfare.
If the Church claims no right to coerce the conscience of the
individual, on what ground does the nation claim such a right?
If, on account of personal human dignity, conscience is held
inviolable in the first instance, why, on grounds of strict logic,
is it not held inviolable in the second?[78]

Would it be an over-simplification of the issue to note that
Cardinal Spellman's stand on religious liberty accorded with
American democratic ideals (for freedom of religion forms
part of the American way of life), and, in the second instance,
his stand on conscientious objection (even though it could
be interpreted as a violation of those same democratic ideals[79])
evidently still accorded with his own interpretation of the
American way? His position on conscientious objection, illogi-
cal as it may seem, is still in the tradition of loyal and
uncritical support by the American Catholic hierarchy of the
nation's wartime needs.[80] It is in the tradition of Archbishop
Carroll, who put aside his own doubts about America's position in the War of 1812, to identify her enemy with the powers
of darkness; it is in the tradition of Archbishop Hughes, who
during the Civil War proclaimed that "there is but one rule
for a Catholic, wherever he is," and that is to fight on the side
where he finds himself;[81] it is in the tradition of Archbishop
Ireland and Cardinal Gibbons, who evidently unthinkingly
supported what they considered an unjust war; of Archbishop
Ireland whose warlike ardor made him refuse "to make a
gospel of peace"; of Cardinal Gibbons who demanded "absolute and unreserved obedience" to the nation's call. And,
above all, it is in the tradition of American Catholics whose
loyalty to the nation must always be demonstrated once again
by prompt, enthusiastic participation in the nation's wars.

From one perspective, Cardinal Spellman's stand could be
viewed as a case of "culture lag." The idea of obedience has
been reviewed both in the Church, in general, and in religious

life, in particular; and in this the modern era, few theologians would defend the ecclesiastical or religious superior's right to demand "absolute and unreserved obedience." But the nation's right to make such a demand on its citizens has not been subjected to the same sort of review, and, for a large number of Catholics, it still stands as unconditional.[82]

## NOTES

[1] Ireland, *The Church and Modern Society*, p. 370.

[2] *Ibid.*, p. 152. These words which Archbishop Ireland used, in referring to the supreme emergency of the Civil War, find their echo in the words of Theodore Roosevelt who saw the Spanish-American War as the same kind of patriotic opportunity which was able to assure the nation "that the power and vitality of the nation were not waning" (Niebuhr and Heimert, *A Nation So Conceived*, p. 130).

[3] Browne, "Catholicism in the United States" in Smith and Jamison, *Religion in American Life*, p. 77.

[4] *Ibid.*, p. 78.

[5] Quoted by Guilday, *The Life and Times of John Carroll*, pp. 81–82.

[6] Browne, *op. cit.*, p. 77.

[7] Guilday, *op. cit.*, p. 113.

[8] Melville, *John Carroll of Baltimore*, p. 87; Guilday, *ibid.*, p. 368.

[9] Melville, *ibid.*, pp. 272–273.

[10] *Ibid.*, p. 273.

[11] *Ibid.*, p. 274.

[12] *Ibid.*, p. 275. In a letter to Father Plowden, dated October 13, 1815, he wrote: "The glory of your country is at its highest elevation. To have stood alone against an overwhelming power, which compelled submission from every power in Europe until it was met by British arms, and to have at length reanimated the trembling nations to shake off their yoke, is the exclusive merit of Englishmen, as His Holiness truly compliments them in his letter to the Bishops of Ireland."— Guilday, *op. cit.*, p. 809.

[13] Archbishop Carroll was not the last of the bishops to "baptize"

the American cause by identifying the enemy with the powers of darkness.

14 Browne, *op. cit.*, p. 85.

15 Peter Guilday, *A History of the Councils of Baltimore (1791–1884)*, p. 153.

16 *Complete Works of the Most Rev. John Hughes*, II, p. 131.

17 Whether Herberg is right (see Chapter 1) that the basic identification of American Catholics is as *Americans*, it would seem true that this is the basic identification which Archbishop Hughes took for granted and applauded during wartime.

18 Guilday, *ibid.*, pp. 169–170.

19 Hassard, *Life of Hughes*, p. 439.

20 *Works*, II, p. 157. The passage continues: "But no matter how wide or how deep they may in their political aspirations and schemes contrive to present the chasm dividing the North from the South, or how impassable, the Catholics on both sides of the line, though they may not be very distinguished engineers, will, as far as religion is concerned, throw a bridge over that chasm." The implication seems to be that, even though it is their duty to fight for their respective side, the bond as fellow Catholics will still remain.

21 Hassard, *ibid.*, p. 451.

22 *Ibid.*, pp. 436–437. Evidently it was not only Hughes who remembered that the abolitionists tended to be anti-Catholic. Guilday remarks (*op. cit.*, p. 187) that "the anti-Catholic and Abolition movements may be said to have walked hand-in-hand." Hughes as a seminarian wrote an impassioned poem against slavery (Hassard, *op. cit.*, p. 40); but as a bishop he seemed to take a much more tolerant view of it and became more incensed at abolitionists than at the institution of slavery itself (*ibid.*, p. 435). Elsewhere he said of slavery: "The terrific part of the question is that not only the individuals brought to the American continent or islands are themselves to be slaves, but their posterity, in like manner for all time to come. This is the only terrible feature about American slavery. And yet it is not alien from the condition of mankind in general. Original sin has entailed upon the human race its consequence for time and eternity. And yet the men who are living now had no part in the commission of original sin" (*ibid.*, p. 436).

23 *The Life of Archbishop Hughes*, p. 19. Hughes' funeral is described in great detail as a "mark of respect paid to his memory which

has never been accorded to any other ecclesiastic in this country since the Declaration of Independence—" all public offices were closed; the flags were at half-mast, etc. (*ibid.*, p. 42).

[24] Browne, *op. cit.*, p. 85.

[25] Thomas F. Meehan, "Catholic Activities in Our Two Great Wars," *Catholic World*, CVII, 640, July 1918, p. 448.

[26] *Ibid.*, p. 451.

[27] *Ibid.*, p. 452.

[28] *Ibid.*, p. 453.

[29] Moynihan, *The Life of Archbishop John Ireland*, p. 7.

[30] John Gilmary Shea, *The Cross and the Flag*, p. 97.

[31] Moynihan, *ibid.*, p. 49.

[32] *Ibid.*, p. 52, quoting Klein, *In the Land of the Strenuous Life* (Chicago: A. C. McClurg, 1915), pp. 332–333.

[33] Ireland, *op. cit.*, p. 172.

[34] *Ibid.*, p. 143.

[35] It is from this speech that the quotation used at the beginning of this chapter is taken: "It is good for a people that supreme emergencies arise to test its patriotism to the highest pitch." See footnote 2.

[36] *Ibid.*, p. 162.

[37] Moynihan, *ibid.*, pp. 50–51.

[38] Moynihan's book was published in 1953. It is difficult to disentangle the biographer's sentiments from Archbishop Ireland's own, and there might be basis for the criticism that Moynihan is projecting his own sentiments onto Ireland, were it not that in the latter's own book the sentiments are much the same.

[39] *Loc. cit.* These are remarkable words to read in the era of *Pacem in Terris*!

[40] Shea, *op. cit.*, p. 77. These words are quoted from a sermon preached by the Rev. Walter Elliott at the Paulist Fathers Church in New York, May 29, 1898. Among other passages from the sermon quoted by Shea are the following:

This war, thank God, with its unitive force, has given the final notes to the sweet hymn of peace which began so plaintively when Robert E. Lee surrendered his stainless sword to Ulysses S. Grant. . . .

We are for war in the interest of peace . . . No race hatred shall profane the sacred cause of this nation, a nation which is the divine blending of the blood of all nations. And whatever territory shall be gained by our valor . . . let us treat our acquisition and their inhabitants as being set over them by the Great Father of Battles in *loco parentis*.

[41] Shea, *ibid.*, p. 80.

[42] *Loc. cit.*

[43] *Ibid.*, p. 85.

[44] *Ibid.*, p. 87.

[45] *Ibid.*, p. 85. Among other sermons quoted by Shea is one of Archbishop Gross of Oregon who, talking of the "more solid gains" of the war beside those "islands that will be of untold value to the interests of our republic," said:

There are shown how deep, how self-sacrificing, how universal is the love and devotion of its citizens for this republic . . .

. . . we rejoice that our country has shown itself a Christian people . . . thanking Him as the arbiter of nations. Aboard ship, while guns still reeked from the just completed victory, officers called their willing crews—and the voice of prayer and thanksgiving arose from the brave veterans to the one true God. And our government gave the many infidel governments of Europe a lesson (*Ibid.*, pp. 86–87).

At Archbishop Corrigan's Silver Jubilee, in May 1898, Bishop McQuaid spoke on "Our Country."

A child of this great city of New York, I feel that love of country down to the very marrow of my bones . . . We want a country unshackled by the chains of European customs . . . I believe in an army that will embrace all the people, which will enable us to defy the world, and in time of war to call not a million but ten million men into the field. Then shall we be able to dictate to Europe and the world the doctrine of peace (*Ibid.*, p. 78).

Shea quotes Bishop Byrne of Nashville as having remarked about the War: "Whatever may have been the individual judgment of Americans prior to the moment when war broke out as to its wisdom or the adequacy of the reasons advanced in its justification, there can be now no two opinions as to the duty of every loyal American citizen" (*ibid.*, p. 77). Although obviously less enthusiastic about the War than Archbishop Gross or Bishop McQuaid, Bishop Byrne evidently felt (if Shea's remarks adequately reflect his state of mind) that no citizen had any right to question the nation's stand even if he had doubts about the justice of its cause.

While Shea quotes no Catholic bishop in the United States who did not support the War, evidently at least one refused to support it. When the appointment as Archbishop of Manila was offered to (the later Cardinal) William O'Connell, he wrote to Rome declining, "Inasmuch as he had not concealed, from the beginning of the Spanish-American War his sympathy for Spain and had openly stated the war was unjust, he had been openly criticized as lacking in patriotism." From a letter

of William O'Connell to Cardinal Rampolla, April 20, 1903, in the
Vatican Archives, as quoted by Dorothy A. Wayman, *Cardinal O'Connell of Boston* (New York: Farrar, Straus and Young, 1955), p. 108.

[46] Ellis, *The Life of James Cardinal Gibbons*, II, p. 91.

[47] *Ibid.*, II, p. 86.

[48] *Ibid.*, II, pp. 86–87.

[49] *Ibid.*, II, p. 90.

[50] *Ibid.*, II, p. 139.

[51] *The National Pastorals of the American Hierarchy*, p. 235. Statement of the Third Plenary Council, 1884.

[52] Will, *Life of Gibbons*, II, p. 813.

[53] *Ibid.*, II, pp. 813–814.

[54] Ellis, *ibid.*, II, p. 239.

[55] *Ibid.*, II, p. 247.

[56] *Loc. cit.* "Church and state amicably move in parallel lines, helping one another in their respective field of labor," was another statement which Cardinal Gibbons made on this occasion. Evidently this is
another instance of the Cardinal's inability to see that there might
possibly be times and issues in which loyalty to higher principles could
interfere with the nation's own definition of what loyalty to itself
demanded.

[57] *Ibid.*, II, p. 259.

[58] *Ibid.*, II, p. 249. Cardinal Gibbons and Archbishop Ireland were,
of course, not the only members of the hierarchy aware that Catholic
patriotism was on display. On March 2, 1918, in speaking on "Catholics and the War," Cardinal Farley asked rhetorically: "Is there a single
thing that Catholics could do for their country which they have not
done?" (Meehan, *op. cit.*, p. 463).

In their 1919 statement, the hierarchy of the United States declared:
"The prediction has been fulfilled. The traditional patriotism of our
Catholic people has been amply demonstrated in the day of their country's trial. And we look with pride upon the record which proved, as
no mere protestation could prove, the devotion of American Catholics
to the cause of American freedom" (*National Pastorals*, p. 295).

[59] Will, *op. cit.*, II, p. 829.

[60] Spellman, *The Road to Victory*, p. 18.

[61] *Ibid.*, p. 20.

[62] *Ibid.*, p. 21.

[63] *Ibid.*, p. 89.

[64] *Ibid.*, pp. 122–123.

[65] *The Risen Soldier* (New York: Macmillan, 1944), p. 2.

[66] *Ibid.*, pp. 38–39.

[67] *The Foundling*, p. 279. Cardinal Spellman does not note here that the war ended on another feast of Our Lady, August 15th.

[68] *Prayers and Poems*, p. 9.

[69] *The Road to Victory*, p. 128. Spellman repeatedly uses the American flag as symbolic of Christian values. The author is indebted to Professor Werner Stark for pointing out that the presence of the national flag, habitual in Catholic churches in the United States, is not found in European countries.

[70] *Risen Soldier*, p. 6.

[71] *What America Means to Me*, p. 5.

[72] It should be noted that what seemed a clear-cut issue of Communism elicited the unambiguous support of American Catholics who, in the two World Wars, had been tempted to hew to an isolationist line. Thomas F. O'Dea remarks that: "the conservatism of Catholic thought and the ethnic loyalties of the Irish and Germans, reinforced by their status in local American communities, tended to align Catholic sentiment against the basic line that was developing in American foreign relations (before World War I). The American Catholic Experience did not prepare American Catholics on the whole to look with favor on a foreign policy friendly to Liberalism and revolution, Anglophile, and, at the same time, antagonistic toward Germany. A tendency for Catholics to align themselves with isolationism was quite understandable under the circumstances" ("American Catholics and International Life," *Social Order*, X, 6, June 1960, p. 255). The tendency toward isolationism before the wars may have resulted in the over-reaction of uncritical and enthusiastic Catholic support of the two World Wars once the nation had entered the fight.

[73] Spellman, *ibid.*, p. 14.

[74] *Ibid.*, p. 11.

[75] *Loc. cit.*

[76] In the third session of the Council, Bishop Philip Hannan, then Auxiliary of Washington, spoke out against the section of the draft of Schema 13 which condemned the use of nuclear weapons as a deterrent. In an article prepared for Bishop Hannan by members of the

Catholic Association of International Peace and given in the CAIP News of October, 1964, William V. O'Brien contended that the Council was in no position to make an authoritative or irrefutable statement on the nuclear deterrent and if it did so, "It would place close to fifty million American Catholics in an awesome dilemma as to whether to listen to the solemn findings of a Vatican Council or to the hitherto accepted assurances of their government . . ." It is obvious that for Bishop Hannan, as well as for the Committee of the CAIP, the dilemma should not be resolved but avoided.

[77] As reported in *Commonweal*, LXXXIII, 1, October 8, 1965, p. 7.

[78] Monsignor George Higgins wrote in a syndicated column in the Catholic diocesan weeklies: ". . . it must be said that the principle of conscientious objection is not only basically sound, but, given the nature of modern warfare and the inevitable power of modern governments, ought to be defended more vigorously today than ever before in human history" (*Commonweal, ibid.*). See also CAIP News, July-Aug. 1965.

[79] The law of the land recognizes the right of conscientious objection on religious grounds and the Supreme Court of the United States has upheld this right, giving an increasingly wide interpretation to the term "religious."

[80] The *Commonweal* editor notes (*loc. cit.*) that "Perhaps Cardinal Spellman, as head of the military ordinariate for U.S. armed forces, is concerned about the rising rate of conscientious objection among Catholics."

[81] Hughes' misgivings about the Civil War, as was pointed out above, do not seem to have revolved around moral principles but possibly around the issue of whether the freeing of the slaves would cause hardship to Irish immigrant labor. Hassard, *op. cit.*, pp. 436–437.

[82] Of course, the Fathers of the Council, in affirming the right of conscientious objection, in reality are questioning this ideology of nationalism and taking a stand against the acceptance of the nation as the final arbiter with the right to coerce the individual's conscience.

# 7/Assessment of Nationalism in American Catholicism

The documentation set forth in the past three chapters seems strongly to suggest that the prelates studied, with the exception of John Lancaster Spalding, did show the influence of the particular American form of national messianism and that the Church leaders did follow along with the spirit of nationalism as it exhibited itself in the relevant periods of the history of the United States. This is not to claim, of course, that they each exhibited the same nationalistic ardor: the measured statements of an Archbishop John Carroll may show none of the ready acceptance of nationalism[1] (in the sense of the definition used throughout this study) that seems so evident in the ebullient orations of an Archbishop John Ireland. But, in one sense, Archbishop Carroll did set the course for whatever nationalism developed in the American Church. A devoted patriot himself, strongly aware of the difficulties that were going to face the tiny, struggling body of Catholics in the newly-independent colonies, the Baltimore prelate did his utmost to see that ecclesiastical institutions would be congruent with American social institutions in general. The very stress on the congruence of the two sets of institutions—initiated by Archbishop Carroll—would mean for some of his successors, at least, disregard of the reality of religious principles as transcending all temporal institutions.

Bishop John England and Archbishop John Hughes, both products of the Irish tradition of nationalism, faced the virulence of the nativist attacks at a time when Catholicism was becoming the single largest religious body in the United States. For them, the apologetic defense of the Church was an all-absorbing task. Although their efforts to prove how Catholic is America suffered from an oftentimes clumsy twisting of history, still they had an effect in encouraging nationalism among American Catholics that is especially paradoxical. As has already been pointed out,[2] Archbishop Hughes was apparently opposed to any effort to adapt the Church to American life, and Catholicism—not Americanism—remained for him the norm of goodness. But implicit in the effort to show how Catholic America is was an attempt to show the identity of the two—Catholicism and Americanism—which would result either in exalting the nation into a transcendental reality or in reducing religion to a temporal equation; but, either way, their efforts promoted the flourishing of nationalism.

The growth of the spirit of nationalism among American Catholics seems to have become more obvious in the time of Cardinal Gibbons and Archbishop Ireland. Attempting, most directly and overtly, to adapt the Church to American life and to win ready acceptance for Catholics as staunch Americans, these prelates were apparently unaware that, in their steering of the course of the American Church, they faced a series of dilemmas (or, it might perhaps be better to say, one major dilemma which kept manifesting itself in various disguises). Intent on proving how completely American the Catholic Church is, both Archbishop Ireland and Cardinal Gibbons evidently were completely unmindful of the fact that, if this successful identification could be made, it would still not be without pitfalls for the Church which, no one doubts, they truly loved. For them, to be truly Catholic was to be truly American. The identification was easy and quick.

Yet, for the religious man, to hold that the nation is privy to the judgments of God is already to have subscribed to nationalism because, by identifying the claims of the nation with the claims of God, he at least implicitly accepts the nation as ultimate arbiter of human affairs. If Cardinal Gibbons and Archbishop Ireland can be said to have adhered to this sort of nationalism, it can be claimed that Cardinal Spellman is even more overt in identifying the judgments and actions of the American nation with those of God. As the quotations from his published writings and circular letters seem to indicate, the identification of God and the nation seems to have become so close that he appears, for all purposes, unable to write about the one without the other. Cardinal Spellman's acceptance of the messianic mission of America has been complete.

Neither Archbishop Ireland nor Cardinals Gibbons and Spellman give any indication they were aware—as evidently Bishop Spalding was—that the cause of religion and the cause of American democracy had to be disentangled, and that the human situation is so fraught with complexities, of which the policy-maker must be aware, that the election of one course of action is seldom without its ambiguities. That these prelates chose to adapt the Church to American society and to see that Catholicism would take on the forms of American culture does not constitute a course of action to be criticized by the sociologist of religion who expects a religion to reflect the culture in which it is rooted. But the sociologist may ask if, electing that choice, these churchmen were aware of the terms of the choice. And this is where a negative answer seems indicated. It is not a matter of accident that Bishop Spalding—more of an intellectual than Cardinal Gibbons or Archbishop Ireland—should have been aware of the dilemmas of nationalism and should have warned against them. In America, at least, the lack of intellectual life in the Church and the flourishing of the spirit of nationalism seem to be connected; Ireland and Gibbons, gifted orators, as they were judged to be in their time, could not be considered as subtle thinkers. They are criticized here not for making the wrong choice, but for their simplistic thinking. Seeing the evils that would be brought about by what they considered the wrong choice, both prelates were apparently quite unaware of all the consequences of what they viewed as the right choice. As Cardinal Spellman seems to do today, Gibbons and Ireland thought in black-and-white terms only, when they viewed any question that affected the American nation.

### NATIONALITIES OR NATIONALISM

Faced by the nationalities' controversy of the 1880's and 1890's, Archbishop Ireland and Cardinal Gibbons chose to resist strongly the idea of perpetuation of separate nationalisms within the American Church. If Cross's interpretation is correct,[3] they viewed their part in the Cahensly episode not as simply to insure that the Germans would not rule the Church in the United States, but to insure the future of the Church in America—indeed to assure themselves that there would be a Catholic Church in America at all. They saw that the Catholic Church could not exist, split up into separate nationality groupings, each with its own hierarchy. They saw such a division as being not only a practical impossibility— being a threat to the unity of the Church in America as well as a perpetuation of foreign loyalties which they considered intolerable to the American people—but also as being theoretically undesirable. They reasoned that, if the masses of American people were to be converted to the Church, Catholicism must become culturally recognizable to them.

It appears obvious that they saw the threat of the perpetuation of separate nationalities and of corresponding nationalisms. At the same time, it seems doubtful that they saw the threat of the spirit of nationalism that was sweeping across the nation in the "nationalist nineties." Archbishop Ireland, who warned German Catholics forcefully of the danger of foreign nationalism, seemed never to have become aware of the parallel danger of American nationalism. In the actions of some of his German confreres he saw the results of the spirit of ultra-nationalism,[4] but he never recognized what can be fairly called the ultra-nationalism in his own writings and speeches.

Like Archbishop Ireland, Cardinal Gibbons was concerned with keeping the *unity* of the Catholic Church in America; but he was equally obtuse to the threat to her *universality*. Succumbing to American nationalism while combatting vigorously the threat of foreign nationalisms is to fall afoul of the other horn of the dilemma. But there is no evidence that for Archbishop Ireland or Cardinal Gibbons the dilemma actually existed. Glorying in the fact that the Catholic Church was becoming increasingly acceptable in America, they accepted the judgment of the nation perhaps too readily. Forgetting the supra-national, universal character of Catholicism, they found, in the more general approval which Catholicism was winning in America, proof that the Church was fulfilling its mission here. But as the Church has its transcendental aspect, it has its prophetic role, without which it cannot wholly fulfill its mission. The perspective of nationalism inevitably interferes with the perspective of prophecy, for America cannot be viewed as under the judgment of God when the intrinsic righteousness of the nation is taken for granted, and when—to use the words of Cardinal Spellman—America's cause is readily seen to be "ultimately God's cause."

THE SECTARIAN TEMPTATION

Allied to the dilemma of nationalism is another dilemma related to it and, perhaps, even more difficult to analyze. This can be called the sectarian temptation—the temptation of a religious body in a hostile environment, where it forms a small minority, to withdraw from participation in the mainstream of the society and to nourish its inner life, to carry out its own cult, and to obey its own code, unmindful of the activities and purposes of the rest of the world.

We are indebted to the Troeltschian analysis of the distinction between the *sect* and its opposite type of ecclesiastical organization, the *church*,[5] and it may seem surprising that the Catholic Church, example *par excellence* for Troeltsch of the *church,* should have faced in the United States the temptation to give a sectarian response. But as Thomas F. O'Dea remarks, "Coming to America as an immigrant Church entering a Protestant culture, it was forced to make its adaptation in ways that often required a defensive posture. Consequently, it was forced to behave in ways resembling a sectarian response."[6] The relative withdrawal from Protestant and secular society and culture in the United States involved an element of militant opposition on the part of Catholics, and this gave them a sectarian characteristic.

Certainly, in their efforts to relate Catholicism to American culture, and to accommodate the life of the Church to the American scene, the prelates studied here (with the probable exception of Archbishop Hughes[7]) seemed to have been aware of the sectarian temptation and to have guarded against it. Archbishop Carroll, Bishop England, Archbishop Ireland and Cardinal Gibbons, particularly, sought to accommodate the Church to American culture and to participate themselves— and to urge participation by the Catholic people—in the on-going life of American society. In one way, the battle which Cardinal Gibbons and Archbishop Ireland waged against those who wanted to perpetuate foreign nationalisms was a struggle to avoid sectarian status; for, as Father Barry brings out rather clearly, the proponents of German separatism frequently saw American society as evil, or at least dangerously tainted, and therefore they wanted to keep the Catholic faithful in a state of withdrawal.[8] Indeed, most of the struggles of Ireland and Gibbons were with those of their fellow Catholic prelates (the so-called "Conservatives") who did not see that repeated denunciation of American society and refusal to allow the faithful to enter into the mainstream of American life represented a markedly un-ecclesiastical response to the problems of the Church in the United States.[9]

But, it can be asked, if Archbishop Ireland and Cardinal Gibbons saw the danger of the sectarian response, did they realize that the problem of the relationship of Catholicism and American society represented truly a dilemma that was incapable of simple resolution? Given the minority position of the Catholic Church in the United States and the fact that it entered, in the person of the Catholic immigrant, into a society whose culture was to a great degree already formed, could the Church easily function as a *church*? Troeltsch sees that "the Church both stabilizes and determines the social order."[10] Given the actual situation for Catholicism in the United States, the difficulties for the Church to function in such a manner are obvious. If the Church were not going to respond like a sect by withdrawing from the world, if there were no possibility of its "determining the social order," what was the alternative?

It can be suggested that prelates, like Gibbons and Ireland and Spellman, alive to the dangers of the sectarian response, were insufficiently aware that the other alternative open to

Catholicism in America represented the other horn of a dilemma. If the Church would not be content to be a sect, would she—and has she been—content to be a *denomination*?

Actually, as Herberg has pointed out, the existence of denominations reveals the emergence of a common religion.[11] He suggests that while America does not have a church in the Troeltschian sense as an organized institution, it "does possess an overall religious entity . . . and that is the trifaith system of Protestant-Catholic-Jew."[12] This has become the common religion to which the denominations represent a way of belonging.

Herberg's judgment is harsh that this denominational adhesion to the common religion of the American Way of Life represents the furthest stage of secularization.[13] The implied acceptance by conventional religion of this denominational status is obvious to Herberg in the contentment which the religious bodies express with their position in American society. Certainly, the Catholic prelates studied here would not have given conscious assent to the reduction of Catholicism to the status of a denominational variant of a common religion. But, one might ask, on the basis of the documentation presented in Chapters 4, 5 and 6, were they so anxious to be accepted by the nation, to have Catholicism considered acceptable within the American social framework, that they were too *accepting*—too accepting of American national goals and values, and, at the same time, too accepting of the subsidiary status that became theirs as one of the American denominations? The documentation educed, while it does not prove the Herberg thesis that Catholicism has become subsumed in the tripartite American religion, does suggest that the prelates studied were more successful in avoiding the sectarian temptation than they were in circumventing tacit acceptance of the denominational position.[14]

## ALIENATION OR COMMITMENT?

Another dilemma, which is, in reality, an aspect of the previous one discussed, is the dilemma of choosing to be alienated or committed to the temporal order and to the society in which a religious group finds itself. Consistent with the election to follow the sectarian response would be the choice of withdrawing from participation in the world, of accepting a state of alienation from the goals and purposes and means and work of a society. Obviously, prelates like Ireland or Gibbons, working to make the Catholic Church "at home" in American society, chose commitment, and they did their best to avoid all behavior that would alienate the Church from society[15] or allow Catholics to remain an alien element on the American scene.

But did the very commitment to the society in which they found themselves keep them from recognizing the evils—the moral and social problems—of that society? Going ahead with what they felt were the goals and aspirations of the society, did they accept it as it was and fail to judge it and transcend it? Accommodating themselves to American society, moved by the urge to be accepted as truly "American," were they too accepting of the society as they found it, and thus did they forget to measure it by a moral yardstick which transcended that used by the nation itself? The seeming acquiescence of the American Catholic prelates to the institution of slavery and to the *status quo* of capitalistic industrialism seems to suggest as much. The fact that Archbishop Ireland and Cardinal Gibbons, in their writings and speeches, urged on the faithful the acceptance of the Protestant ethic (insofar as they stressed, as virtues to be developed, the "American" traits of sobriety, thrift and initiative) would suggest their own uncritical commitment to American society as they found it.[16]

Given the minority status of American Catholics and the defensive, often pitiful, condition in which they found themselves, it is understandable why there would be an avoidance of issues that would cause a painful confrontation with the majority of which they were struggling to become a part. It is understandable, too, that the statements issued by the plenary and provincial council meetings of the hierarchy should have been singularly lacking in the discussion of national issues, other than those which affected the Church and its institutional concerns in a direct fashion.[17] Indeed, it was not until 1919 that the hierarchy assembled in their annual meeting issued a statement that was notable for the fact that—while it revealed a wholehearted commitment to American society—it gave incisive, insightful criticism of the evils of this society and did not hesitate to sketch a program of social reforms.[18] But even this statement is more notable for the way it handled domestic social problems than for the way it handled America's part in international life.[19] It would seem that the same unthinking acceptance of the nation's own definition of its role which marked the response of the American hierarchy in wartime has led it to remain silent on the nation's part in international affairs in time of peace.

To be committed to a society does not necessarily mean that one should see only the good things in that society. Yet, while it is understandable that the recent immigrant should hesitate to criticize the society of which he so ardently desires to become a part, the habit of uncritical acceptance, once it has developed, is difficult indeed to break. The bishops who have figured in this study, with the exception of Archbishop Carroll and Bishop Spalding of immigrant background, did show that ardent desire to be given an American identity. It is not surprising, then, that they should have failed to be outspoken in their judgment of the evils of American society, nor that unthinking commitment, in the main, to its way of life should have paralleled unthinking acceptance of the spirit of nationalism.

## NOTES

[1] His statements during the War of 1812, in their espousal of nationalism, are not typical of his tone at other times.

[2] Chapter 4.

[3] See Chapter 3.

[4] Chapter 3.

[5] Ernst Troeltsch, *The Social Teachings of the Christian Churches*, Olive Wyon, tr., (New York: Harper Torchbooks, 1960), Vol. I & II.

[6] Thomas F. O'Dea, "American Catholics and International Life," *Social Order*, p. 248.

[7] Archbishop Hughes seemed to have assumed more of a defensive posture and to stress a great deal more militant opposition to American society. Yet, even in the words and actions of Hughes, there is evidence of elements that would incline him to avoid the sectarian response and to participate in the larger society.

[8] Barry, O.S.B., *The Catholic Church and German Americans*.

[9] Cross, *The Emergence of Liberal Catholicism in America*.

[10] Troeltsch, *op. cit.*, I, p. 331.

[11] Herberg, "Religion in a Secularized Society," in Schneider, *Religion, Culture and Society*, p. 593. "Obviously, the denominational system implies the emergence of a 'common religion' distinct from the conventional religion of the denominations, for without such a 'common religion' the society in which the denominations find their place in mutual legitimation would hardly be able to hold together."

[12] *Ibid.*, p. 595.

[13] *Loc. cit.*

[14] Obviously it is a theological problem, outside the scope of this study, how Catholicism will function in a world where—on a world-wide basis—like all of Christianity, it is increasingly a minority religion. However, the sociologist is free to speculate on the possibility of a new form emerging, alongside the sociological types of the

"church," the "sect," and the "denomination," which will allow the Catholic Church to function in the world and yet keep to the fore its unique claims, especially its claim of transcending the society in which it finds itself.

[15] In the forefront of Cardinal Gibbons' motivation, in his stand on such issues as the Knights of Labor and the doctrines of Henry George, was the fear that Vatican condemnation would mean alienation of Catholicism from American society.

[16] These two prelates have had the reputation of being more progressive on social issues than many of their contemporaries in the hierarchy. Yet Ireland's speeches are as much marked by an uncritical acceptance of capitalism as they are by his enthusiastic assent to the concept of Manifest Destiny. Gibbons' defense of the Knights of Labor did not reveal him to be aware of the larger social problems of industrial capitalism. Several times he is quoted by his biographers, Ellis and Will, as pointing out the evils in American society, but these passages (at least from our present vantage-point) seem singularly lacking in astute social criticism. Thus, in 1889, he wrote: "We are confronted by five great evils—Mormonism and divorce, which strike at the root of the family and society; an imperfect and vicious system of education, which undermines the religion of our youth; the desecration of the Christian Sabbath, which tends to obliterate in our adult population the salutary fear of God and the homage we owe Him; the gross and systematic election frauds; and lastly the unreasonable delay in carrying into effect the sentences of our criminal courts . . ." He sees "every other moral and social delinquency" (including the discontent of the poor) as being traceable "to one of the five radical vices enumerated above" (Will, *Life of Gibbons*, II, p. 896). As late as 1906—a good fifteen years after the issuing of *Rerum Novarum*—Cardinal Gibbons enumerated, as the three great evils of the day, "suicide, divorce, and Communism" (*Ibid.*, II, p. 680).

[17] *The National Pastorals of the American Hierarchy (1792–1919).*

[18] Raphael M. Huber, ed., *Our Bishops Speak (1919–1951)* (Milwaukee: Bruce, 1952).

[19] The 1919 statement reiterates the bishops' pride in the proven loyalty of the American Catholics during World War I, and seems to reflect still the need to prove that Catholics are good Americans.

# 8/The Fusion of Religion with Nationalism in the Pluralist Society

*"Every functioning society has, to an important degree, a common religion. The possession of a common set of ideas, rituals, and symbols can supply an overarching sense of unity even in a society riddled with conflict."*[1]

The nationalism of the American Catholic bishops cannot be understood without taking into consideration the background factors of Irish nationalism, the nativist movement, and the nationalities' controversy. The push toward a fusion of religion with nationalism which we contend was present already in pluralistic America was facilitated, in the case of American Catholics, by the presence of three factors. The Irish nationalism in the background of the Catholic bishops, which had allowed them to identify their Irishness with their Catholicism, permitted them to make a ready transference to the American scene, and—as Herberg has indicated and we have discussed in Chapter 3—to identify their Americanism with their Catholicism. It can be noted that the bishops were especially disposed to taking a nationalistic stance because, while they were able after a time to accept the pluralism of the American nation, they seemed unable to accept the nation as being truly *secular*. Therefore, they felt themselves under the onus of proving its congruence with Catholicism. The inability to accept the nation as secular meant, furthermore, that the bishops tended to enfold America and Americanism in an atmosphere of the sacred which meant, in turn, that the nation became identified with the religious commitment instead of being itself brought under the judgment of religion. For it is only when the nation is viewed as being really secular that it is not confused with the transcendental object of religion, but rather is viewed, in all its relativity, as being under the judgment of God.[2] With the background of their Irish nationalism giving to their adherence to the American nation and its national goals some of the aura of the sacred, the bishops were not disposed to view the nation as truly secular. As a consequence, they were prepared for a commitment to nationalism.

The nativist movement is the second distinctive feature to be taken into consideration in the study of nationalism in American Catholicism. That the hostility of the nativists provoked a defensive reaction on the part of the Catholic immigrant is evident. Accused of harboring foreign allegiances, the Catholics reacted by reaffirming their commitment to the American nation. Archbishop Ireland, who beat the A.P.A. at their own game of one-hundred-per-cent patriotism, may have been an extreme example, but there is no doubt that his protestations of national loyalty were the typical response of the member of the minority group under heavy attack by the majority. Certainly the nativist movement expedited the development of nationalism on the part of these Catholic immigrants whose integration into American society had so severely been called into question.

Finally, the nationalities' controversy was the circumstance which apparently evoked an unquestioning commitment to the goals and the aims of the American nation. Its importance for an understanding of nationalism in American Catholicism cannot be over-stressed. Indeed, for Archbishop Ireland and Cardinal Gibbons, the nationalities' controversy appears to have been crucial in shaping their response to American nationalism, and especially in disposing them to accept the spirit of the "nationalist nineties." But apparently the nationalities' controversy remained a potent, present memory in the American Church years after the particular crisis of Cahenslyism had been resolved. The accusation—or possibility of accusation—of adherence to any foreign nationalism lingered on among the members of the American Catholic hierarchy, who, in the critical periods of war especially, found in it impetus to reaffirm their Americanism in extravagant terms.

The nature of American nationalism itself was certainly a factor in expediting the development of nationalism among the American Catholic bishops.[3] As Tocqueville pointed out, in America the notion of Christianity and civil liberty were combined, and religion and liberty were seen also as moving in the same direction in the United States. In Europe, he noted, religion and democracy were viewed as enemies; in America, they were friends. In this political climate, congenial to religion, it is no wonder that the Catholic bishops felt little cause to question the spirit of nationalism. The ambiguities between religion and nationalism in the United States could easily be overlooked, once it was established that they were, indeed, firm friends.

But do Irish nationalism, nativism, and the nationalities' controversy fully account for the presence of nationalism in American Catholicism? Put another way, would nationalism have developed anyway in American Catholicism even if these circumstantial factors had not been present? We are disposed to answer in the affirmative for reasons which we shall now explain.

First, let us note a facile popular explanation of the supposed nationalism of American Catholics. This would account for the phenomenon as simply a result of Catholic immigration to a predominantly Protestant country—a vividly noticeable result, but a transitory one. This explanation rests on the premise that, when American Catholics feel completely assimilated, any noticeable nationalism in American Catholicism will disappear.

Actually, such an explanation is allied to Herberg's more highly developed and cogent explanation of the co-existence of traditional religion and nationalism in the United States. Admitting the viability of religions in America and the number of their adherents—particularly since the claimed "religious revival" of the fifties—Herberg nevertheless maintains his thesis that the American Way of Life has become the common religion. He attempts to explain this apparent paradox on the basis of the American immigrant experience. Following the so-called "third-generation hypothesis,"[4] he argues that the grandchildren of immigrants, who can no longer look to the ethnic group for support either in giving them a sense of identity or in tying them into the larger society, have looked toward religion to fulfill these functions. So it is that in Protestantism, Catholicism, or Judaism, they find an acceptable way of subscribing to the American creed and following the American Way of Life. As a consequence, they swell the ranks of the traditional religions while they become greater devotees of the "common religion."

Both sociologists and religionists have been greatly attracted by Herberg's thinking, but they have tended to focus on either of two components in it: they have argued as to whether or not the grandchildren of immigrants are indeed more religious than the sons of immigrants;[5] or they have argued whether or not there has, indeed, been a religious revival at all.[6] Both of these questions, it is suggested, may have served to sidetrack the more important issue that Herberg raises: the *theory* behind the coexistence of religion and nationalism in America and the peculiar admixture of the two in the culture of the United States.[7]

This phenomenon, to which Herberg attracted attention over the past decade, seems to be the same phenomenon which absorbed Tocqueville's attention at the time of his visit to the United States. It is the present writer's contention that the explanation of American religiosity and nationalistic fervor on the basis of immigration is called into question by the writings of Tocqueville, whose journey to this country in 1830 antedated the great waves of immigration. At that time, when the population of the United States was relatively homogenous compared to what it was to become later, Tocqueville noted the intense patriotism combined with extreme religiosity among the Americans, and in his writings can be found, at least in seminal form, a theory of the relationship between nationalism and religion in a pluralist society. As Tocqueville was profoundly aware, the United States, as the first pluralist democracy, had to achieve its integration in a way for which history provided no pattern.

Pursuing Tocqueville's line of thought, then, the question presents itself: Are there problems concerning the relationship of religion and nationalism which are intrinsic to the nature of the pluralist society, and from which we have been sidetracked by the important, but nonetheless extrinsic, factor of mass immigration in the case of the United States? This question provokes an examination of the nature of a pluralist society, a society that lacks a common religion.

## TOWARD THE DEVELOPMENT OF A THEORY

What happens when men, with fully deliberate intent— perhaps out of expediency or in order to foster other values which they have come to esteem—found a nation which excludes the establishment of a common religion (as was the case in the foundation of the United States), a nation which, in other words, is expected to function on a pluralistic basis? Sociological theorists who, like Talcott Parsons, follow Emile Durkheim[8] have been concerned to analyze those functions or consequences which a common religion has for a society. They have seen the fundamental importance of religious ideas in providing the basis for a society's understanding of itself and its common ultimate values and goals, as well as the importance of the religious cult in symbolizing and promoting a sense of common identity. A pluralist society, however, rules out the possibility of a common religion existing to provide a people with a common cognitive orientation from which to view the world as well as the common symbols to reinforce their sense of social solidarity. No one religion provides common value orientations for the *whole* of life or uses symbols which can express *fully* the collective sentiments.

But if Parsons is correct that a common cognitive orientation, an accepted system of ultimate values and goals, and a means to assure effective social integration are necessary for a society's successful functioning, what happens when these are missing? If the people of a society lack a system of common sacred objects, which at the same time express and stimulate their sense of solidarity, how will they supply the lack? In the absence of a common religion, will a substitute be found?

It is suggested here that in the pluralistic society of the United States there is a peculiar blending of nationalism and religion to form an amalgam which serves as a *common religion*. In order for the different religions to survive, they must support a common value system, and this union of nationalism and traditional religion provides a substitute for the system of common sacred objects which the pluralistic society lacks. It is toward this fusion of nationalism and religion that the

people of the pluralistic society look for the source of their
unity, for the symbols to uphold and reaffirm their common
identity, and, in a word, to supply for the lack of a common
religion and to become, by substitution, *the* common religion.

An examination of the actual historical experience of the
development of pluralism in the United States is crucial to
the investigation of a theory of the union of nationalism and
religion to form a substitute for a common religion. In Chapter 2 we examined the relationship of religion and nationalism
from the time of the foundation of the nation. Focusing especially on the development of the American sense of mission,
we saw that the particular American form of national messianism was brought about by the convergence of political
with religious ideas of destiny; it seemed impossible to conceive of one without the other. Evidence was presented to
suggest that the same development which made for religious
pluralism in America also made for the religiosity of Americans. Religion was seen to be at the core of American values
and to provide agreement about ultimate national values, as
well as about the ultimate meaning of the nation. This convergence of religion with political and social ideas of national
destiny and mission formed a consensus of values that apparently was present from the beginning of our nation. In that
sense, at least, we already had a *common religion* at the time
of our national birth.[9] While this "common religion" did not
have the tripartite expression which was to come later, at its
heart it seems to have been the same phenomenon noted by
Herberg. As in the case of Benjamin Franklin, religion (in
the conventional sense) was already emptied of specific religious content and was put at the service of nationalism.
Evidence suggests that, even at the time of the foundation
of the United States, there already existed Herberg's American
of "great faith"[10]—a faith, however, whose specific content

was unimportant, but a faith which corroborated and upheld his national loyalty. Religion existed entwined with nationalism to form an ideology of national meaning and destiny. We are now in a position to analyze the more specific characteristics of the relationship between nationalism and conventional religion.

## SUGGESTED RELATIONSHIPS BETWEEN RELIGION AND NATIONALISM IN THE PLURALIST SOCIETY

From our examination of nationalism in American Catholicism, it is possible to suggest the following as hypothetical components of the relationship of religion to nationalism in a pluralist society:

1. *Those elements in the different religions will be stressed which do not impinge on the national value system; those values and norms which show possibility of concordance with the national value system are especially likely to be developed.*

In the lives and writings of Archbishop Ireland and Cardinal Gibbons, in particular, we have viewed attempts to promote a way of life among Catholics in America that would coincide with the American value system. These prelates frequently, in their lectures and sermons, exhorted their hearers to practice virtues which, from the point of view of the Catholic moral code, are distinctly "second-string" (frugality, sobriety, thrift, industry, etc.). The attempt to prove how American is Catholicism was an attempt to put the Catholic Church on record as being in accord with the national value system.

2. *Religion will be used to sanction the nationalist goals, to support them, and to encourage adherence to them.*

At the conclusion of this study, we can make the judgment

that this hypothesis stands as being of prime importance in viewing the relationship of religion to nationalism in the pluralist society. In the attempts to prove the congruence of Americanism and Catholicism, for example, the use of religion to support and sanction nationalist goals has been marked. Religion was put to just those utilitarian uses by the prelates we have studied, especially during periods of war. Only Bishop Spalding seemed aware of the possible perversion of ends and means in the use of religion to serve utilitarian purposes.

3. *There will likely be pruning of any transcendent beliefs of diverse religions to bring about a greater harmony among them through the avoidance of doctrinal controversy. This will allow their adherents to form one national community.*

The liberal wing of the Catholic Church in the United States, at the time of the discussion of the so-called Americanist heresy, was accused of pruning certain Catholic dogmas in order to make the Church more acceptable to American society. While Cardinal Gibbons and Archbishop Ireland insisted that they never held any of the doctrines which were condemned, and while the debate on the issue of Americanism ended rather inconclusively, there remains the possibility that both churchmen, in their efforts to make Catholic teaching acceptable to Americans, had so accommodated themselves to American society that they were truly unaware of the danger of minimizing the importance of certain dogmas. Although in this study there has been no direct demonstration of the "pruning of any transcendental beliefs," such a possibility remains open.[11] It is interesting to note that, up until the present ecumenical era, there is evidence that certain dogmas were stressed which set the Catholic apart from the Protestant. For example, devotion to Our Lady (and the dogmas concerning her) was marked. However, while this tended to give Catholics a specific mark of identity, it did not interfere with the adjustment of Catholics to American life, and, at least in the case of Cardinal Spellman, devotion to Our Lady is used to support nationalistic goals. Evidently the continuance of specific transcendental beliefs does not prevent the formation of one national community as long as there is the common core of values. Growing secularization, moreover, allows people to collaborate in the solution of instrumental problems, whatever they think of the Trinity.

4. *During periods of crisis, when the claims of the nation are in conflict with moral or religious principles, the claims of the nation will be viewed as having prior right.*

The acceptance of, and ready cooperation with, the goals of the United States in the Spanish-American War by Cardinal Gibbons and Archbishop Ireland—even though they considered the war unjust—would seem to stress the importance of this hypothesis and to suggest that it should be given serious consideration in any future study of the conduct of religious leaders in a pluralist society.

5. *Members of the society will look to nationalism rather than to a particular religion for their ultimate identity, sense of social solidarity, and mutual reassurance in the face of external threats. The symbols of nationalism will express their collective personality and excite them to forget themselves in heroic action.*

The writings of Archbishop Ireland and of Cardinal Spellman, in particular, show that they looked toward nationalism to perform these social functions of a common religion. However, there seems to be no evidence that the symbols of nationalism have replaced the symbols of religion in evoking a sense of common personality and in calling forth heroic action; rather, as is clearly evident in those writings of Cardinal Spellman that have been examined, there appears to be a fusion of the two sets of symbols (nationalist and religious) into one.

This hypothetical component of the relationship of religion to nationalism in a pluralist society decidedly calls for further study, since it gets at the crux of the matter: the substitutive power of nationalism fused with religion for the social functions of a common religion.

6. *Religion will have a specific rather than a diffuse role in the pluralist society. It may or may not have many adherents, depending on circumstances specific to the particular society and its culture.*[12] *However, it will tend to be "religion at a very low temperature," to use Robin Williams' expressive phrase.*

In American society, as we have seen, religion has had many adherents, but, in one sense at least, it has tended to be "Sunday religion," not infusing or informing the daily lives of its followers. It has, for example, tended to play a specialized role of sanctioning the standards of the society, rather than transforming or transcending them. Certainly no sufficient evidence has been accumulated to allow us to reach the conclusion that Catholicism in America is indeed "religion at a very low temperature." We have seen, however, that the nationalism present in American Catholicism has had a dampening effect on the prophetic function of religion. And religion without prophecy is religion without fire.

7. *Leaders of a religion will use religion to support nationalism not simply to keep their church acceptable in the pluralist society, but out of the same need for identity and the sense of belonging that motivates all people in the given society.*

This statement apparently finds ratification in the writings of Cardinal Spellman especially; for the Cardinal goes beyond the use of nationalistic symbols for apologetic purposes, as he goes beyond the reiteration of his Americanism simply to

remain acceptable as a Catholic American. If his writings
can be taken at their face value, it is his Americanism which
gives him his identity and reassures him that he belongs to
American society.

## SOME UNANSWERED QUESTIONS

The phenomenon noted by Herberg of the peculiar relationship resulting from the fusion of nationalism and religion in
the United States has, in this study, been traced back to the
beginnings of the United States. It is our contention that this
phenomenon is not transitory (due merely to the effects of
immigration), but belongs rather to the essential functioning
of a pluralist society. A common core of values is a functional
necessity for a pluralist society, and the convergence of religious and political ideas of national mission and destiny,
which took the place of the "common religion" lacking in
pluralistic America, has provided this functional requirement.

But our study has raised more questions than it has answered. Religion, we have seen, is intrinsic to the core of
American values. Can other pluralist societies reach a consensus (have a common core of values) around something
other than religion? And if so, would the relationship between
religion and nationalism take a different form? These questions
will remain unanswered until extensive comparative study of
pluralist societies has been undertaken and completed.

The hypothetical components of the relationship between
religion and nationalism in a pluralist society, which have been
suggested by the analysis of the American Catholic experience,
need to be tested by studying other religious groups in the
United States. Do all religions prominent in American society
exhibit the same uncritical nationalism? In contrast, is marked
deviation from a collective adherence to a common religion
found only among the sects which maintain a pronounced

degree of isolation from the society? These are other questions which merit investigation if we are to come to a fuller understanding of the relationship of religion to nationalism in the pluralist society.

Furthermore, studies in the field of historical sociology are necessary if we are to refine the differences between, on the one hand, the relationship of diverse religions to nationalism in a pluralist society and, on the other hand, the relationship of religion to nationalism in a society with a common religion —or even, for that matter, in a society dominated by a totalitarian government. Very frequently the manifestations of nationalism by religious leaders are the same, however much the types of societies from which they emanate may differ. One could compare, for instance, the writings of the German bishops during the Second World War, as they proclaimed the model Christianity of the soldiers who died for the Fatherland,[13] with the sentiments expressed by Cardinal Spellman who saw the fallen American soldier as "the Risen Christ."[14] Here the expressions of nationalism in a totalitarian society and in a pluralist society are strikingly similar.

However, the underlying difference cannot be neglected. When Cardinal Spellman identified American and Catholic goals, his Americanism with his Catholicism, he was certainly not unaware that Americanism—and the American nation— can exist without Catholicism. Nevertheless, he saw no incompatibility between the two. On the other hand, the German bishops, no matter how much they strove during the Nazi period to show the compatibility of Catholic and German goals, were not unaware of the tension between the two. In contrast, when Archbishop Luis Alonso Munoyerro, Vicar General of the Armed Forces in Spain—a nation with a common religion—speaks out against religious liberty which he views as part of an international plot "to make Catholic unity disappear from our Fatherland,"[15] it is evident that, for the

Spanish archbishop, the nation and its religion really are inseparable.

A typology of relationships between religion and nationalism in different types of societies awaits further development[16]—development which may possibly provide the answer to the basic theoretical question with which we are left: Is it inevitable that Durkheim's *representation collective*—the symbols and values of the nation projected into the heavens and given the status of a divine being—should become the real object of worship, whether or not a society has a common religion in the conventional sense? Of prime importance to the sociologist of religion as well as to the theologian are the questions whether this tribal deity always wars against the claim of a universal God, and whether the transcendental character of religion is always in danger of being submerged by recurrent bouts of tribal self-worship. For this, in the last analysis, is what nationalism becomes. The nation, given the status of final arbiter of human affairs, replaces the God of religion as the final judge of man.

For Americans, the question takes a special twist: Can the secular, pluralist society, which rightly glories in freedom of worship, really allow diversity? Or is a common religion such a fundamental necessity that it, too, will insist on worship of a common deity?

## NOTES

[1] Robin M. Williams, Jr., *American Society: A Sociological Interpretation* (New York: Knopf, 1951), p. 312.

[2] This thought is suggested by Harvey Cox, *The Secular City* (New York: Macmillan, 1965). Cox, noting the biblical sources of secularization, sees it as bringing about a "constructive relativism" which "makes possible a stance by which the national, racial and cultural idolatries

of the age can be put in their place. It allows secular man to note the transience and relativity of all cultural creations . . ." (*Op. cit.*, pp. 32–33).

3 What particular factors in the *personality* of the American Catholic bishops pre-disposed them to nationalism is, of course, outside the scope of this study, which, as an essay in sociology, must remain psychologically open-ended. Freud sees nationalism as related to father-fixation, with its emphasis on the realities of "fatherland," "blood," and "soil." Erich Fromm, in contrast, sees nationalism as allied to mother-fixation. In *The Heart of Man* (New York: Harper and Row, 1964), p. 99, he writes: "Empirically the fact can easily be established that there is a close correlation between persons with a strong fixation to their mothers and those with exceptionally strong ties to nation and race, soil and blood." On p. 106, he notes: "If 'mother' cannot be wrong, how can I judge anyone else objectively if he is in conflict with 'mother' or disapproved by her? This form of impairment of judgment is much less obvious when the object of fixation is not mother but the family, the nation, or the race."

4 Herberg, of course, borrowed this idea from Marcus Lee Hansen who stated it pithily: "What the son tries to forget, the grandson tries to remember."

5 For a good summary of the sociological research done on this question, see Bernard Lazerwitz and Louis Rowitz. "The Three-Generations Hypothesis," *American Journal of Sociology*, LXIX, 5 (March, 1964), pp. 529–538.

6 Seymour M. Lipset, for one, argues against the notion of a "new" religiosity. "While the obvious problems of reliability and validity involved in the use of American church membership statistics make it difficult to reach any conclusions, the available evidence does suggest that, from some time early in American history down to the present, the United States has experienced a continuous 'boom' in religious adherence and belief." *The First New Nation*, p. 144.

7 In all justice to Herberg it should be mentioned that he himself at least suggests a theory relating the two: every functioning society needs a common religion, and, in the United States, the American Way of Life provides it. *Protestant-Catholic-Jew*, p. 74.

8 Emile Durkheim, *The Elementary Forms of the Religious Life* (New York: Collier, 1961).

[9] If this is so, that we already had a common religion at the time of our foundation as a nation, the "dilemma of pluralism" was never really there, and Sidney Mead is wrong in his implications (in *The Lively Experiment*) that, as a nation, we must face up to it. Backhanded evidence that the dilemma does not exist is provided by the fact that only a few persons see the need to teach "secular democracy" or some other variant of a common religion. Evidently, Herberg is right: for most Americans, the American Way of Life is enough of a common religion to which they can adhere through their denominational membership.

[10] Herberg quotes an Eisenhower statement, reported in *The New York Times* of May 4, 1948: "I am the most intensely religious man I know . . . A democracy cannot exist without a religious base. I believe in Democracy."

[11] The blurring of theological differences and the pruning of transcendental beliefs, in order to promote adherence to the "common religion" resulting from the attempted fusion of nationalism and conventional religion, should not, of course, be confused with the sense of common origins and destiny promoted by the ecumenical movement today. As Herberg writes: "Of recent years, we know, there has been a rapprochement, in America as in Europe, between theologically concerned Protestants and Catholics, even between theologically concerned Christians and Jews, precisely as a consequence of their theological concern. It is not the 'common religion' of the American Way that binds them; it is rather their common Christian, their common Biblical, faith and understanding. Indeed, suspicion of the American Way as a substitute-religion serving Americans as their ultimate context of meaning and value is a common premise" ("Religion in a Secularized Society," in Schneider, *Religion, Culture and Society*, p. 598). The ecumenical movement and the religion of the American Way of Life may both owe their origin to the pluralist society (one does not have to be a Marxist to admit at least some influence of the infrastructure on the superstructure); but the one is based on theological concern; the other, on theological indifference.

[12] Available evidence suggests that the so-called "religious revival" of the fifties was idiosyncratic to the United States and does not allow us to generalize that religiosity will be a mark of the emerging pluralist nations.

13 Gordon Zahn, *German Catholics and Hitler's Wars* (New York: Sheed and Ward, 1961), p. 94. See also Guenter Lewy, *The Catholic Church and Nazi Germany* (New York: McGraw-Hill, 1964).

14 Francis J. Spellman, *The Risen Soldier.*

15 *The New York Times,* December 18, 1964.

16 An attempt to develop a typology of relationships between religion and nationalism in different kinds of societies can be found in Dorothy Dohen, *The Social Functions of Nationalism and Religion in a Pluralist Society* (Fordham University, unpublished doctoral dissertation, 1966).

# Bibliography

## BOOKS

Bailey, Thomas A. *The American Spirit*. 2 vols. Boston: Heath, 1963.

Baltzell, E. Digby. *The Protestant Establishment*: Aristocracy and Caste in America. New York: Random House, 1964.

Baron, Salo Wittmayer. *Modern Nationalism and Religion*. New York: Meridian Books, 1960.

Barry, Colman J., O.S.B. *The Catholic Church and German Americans*. Milwaukee: Bruce, 1953.

Bell, Daniel (ed.). *The New American Right*. New York: Criterion Books, 1955.

Bergson, Henri. *The Two Sources of Morality and Religion*. Translated by R. Ashley Audra and Cloudesley Brereton, with the assistance of W. Horsfall Carter. New York: Henry Holt, 1935.

Billington, Ray Allen. *The Protestant Crusade*. New York: Macmillan, 1938.

Bridenbaugh, Carl. *Mitre and Sceptre*: Transatlantic Faiths, Ideas, Personalities and Politics 1689–1775. New York: Oxford University Press, 1962.

Burns, Edward McNall. *The American Idea of Mission*. New Brunswick, N.J.: Rutgers University Press, 1957.

Catholic Association for International Peace. *Patriotism, Nationalism and the Brotherhood of Man*. New York: Paulist Press, 1937.

Cecil, Lord Hugh. *Nationalism and Catholicism*. London: Macmillan, 1919.

Christ, Frank L., and Sherry, Gerard E. (ed.). *American Catholicism and the Intellectual Ideal*. New York: Appleton-Century-Crofts, 1961.

Commager, Henry Steele. *The American Mind*: An Interpretation of American Thought and Character since the 1880's. New Haven: Yale University Press, 1950.

Cox, Harvey. *The Secular City*. New York: Macmillan, 1965.

Cross, Robert D. *The Emergence of Liberal Catholicism in America*. Cambridge, Mass.: Harvard University Press, 1953.

Curti, Merle. *The Roots of American Loyalty*. New York: Columbia University Press, 1946.

Deutsch, Karl. *Interdisciplinary Bibliography in Nationalism*. Cambridge, Mass.: M.I.T. Press, 1956.

————. *Nationalism and Social Communication*: An Inquiry into the Foundations of Nationality. New York: Wiley and M.I.T. Press, 1953.

Devine, M. C. *The World's Cardinal*. Boston: Daughters of St. Paul, 1964.

Drucker, Peter F. *The New Society*. New York: Harper, 1950.

Durkheim, Emile. *The Elementary Forms of the Religious Life*. Translated by Joseph Ward Swain. New York: Collier, 1961.

Earle, Edward Mead (ed.). *Nationalism and Internationalism*: Essays Inscribed to Carlton J. H. Hayes. New York: Columbia University Press, 1950.

Eliade, Mircea. *The Sacred and the Profane*: The Nature of Religion. New York: Harcourt, Brace, 1959.

Ellis, John Tracy (ed.). *Documents of American Catholic History*. Milwaukee: Bruce, 1962.

————. *John Lancaster Spalding*. Milwaukee: Bruce, 1961.

————. *The Life of James Cardinal Gibbons*. 2 vols. Milwaukee: Bruce, 1952.

Emerson, Rupert. *From Empire to Nation*. Cambridge, Mass.: Harvard University Press, 1960.

England, John. *The Works of the Right Rev. John England.* Collected and arranged by the Right Rev. Ignatius A. Reynolds. 5 vols. Baltimore: Murphy, 1849.

Fichter, Joseph H., S.J. *Are We Going Secular?* Milwaukee: Marquette University Press, 1960.

Frazer, Sir James George. *The Golden Bough.* New York: Macmillan, 1927.

Fromm, Erich. *The Heart of Man.* New York: Harper and Row, 1964.

Gannon, Robert I., S.J. *The Cardinal Spellman Story.* Garden City, N.Y.: Doubleday, 1962.

Gerth, Hans H., and Mills, C. Wright. *Character and Social Structure.* New York: Harcourt, Brace, 1954.

Ginsberg, Morris. *Nationalism: a Reappraisal.* Leeds: Leeds University Press, 1961.

Glazer, Nathan, and Moynihan, Daniel Patrick. *Beyond the Melting Pot.* Cambridge, Mass.: M.I.T. Press, 1963.

Goode, William J. *Religion among the Primitives.* Glencoe, Ill.: Free Press, 1951.

Gordon, Milton M. *Assimilation in American Life*: The Role of Race, Religion, and National Origins. New York: Oxford University Press, 1964.

Gould, J., and Kolb, W. L. (ed.). *Dictionary of the Social Sciences.* New York: The Free Press, 1964.

Grant, Robert M. *The Sword and the Cross.* New York: Macmillan, 1955.

Guilday, Peter. *A History of the Councils of Baltimore (1791–1884).* New York: Macmillan, 1932.

————. *The Life and Times of John Carroll.* New York: The Encyclopedia Press, 1922.

————. *The Life and Times of John England.* 2 vols. New York: The America Press, 1927.

Haselden, Kyle, and Marty, Martin E. *What's Ahead for the Churches?* New York: Sheed and Ward, 1964.

Hassard, John R. G. *Life of the Most Rev. John Hughes.* New York: Appleton, 1866.

Hayes, Carlton J. H. *Essays on Nationalism.* New York: Macmillan, 1926.

Hayes, Carlton J. H. *The Historical Evolution of Modern Nationalism.* New York: Macmillan, 1931.

————. *Nationalism: a Religion.* New York: Macmillan, 1960.

Hecker, Isaac T. *The Church and the Age.* New York: Catholic World, 1887.

Herberg, Will. *Protestant-Catholic-Jew.* 2d ed. revised. Garden City, New York: Doubleday Anchor, 1960.

Higham, John. *Strangers in the Land*: Patterns of American Nativism, 1860–1925. New Brunswick, N.J.: Rutgers University Press, 1955.

Hofstadter, Richard. *Anti-Intellectualism in American Life.* New York: Knopf, 1963.

Holtom, Daniel C. *Modern Japan and Shinto Nationalism.* Chicago: University of Chicago Press, 1943.

Huber, Raphael M. (ed.). *Our Bishops Speak (1919–1951).* Milwaukee: Bruce, 1952.

Hughes, John. *The Catholic Chapter in the History of the United States.* New York: Dunigan, 1852.

————. *Christianity the Only Source of Moral, Social and Political Regeneration.* A sermon preached in the Hall of the House of Representatives of the United States, on Sunday, Dec. 12, 1847. New York: Dunigan, 1848.

————. *Complete Works of the Most Rev. John Hughes.* 2 vols. New York: Lawrence Kehoe, 1865.

————. *Letter on the Antecedent Causes of the Irish Famine in 1847.* New York: Dunigan, 1847.

————. *A Letter on the Moral Causes That Have Produced the Evil Spirit of the Times*: Addressed to the Honorable James Harper, Mayor of New York, Including a Vindication of the Author from the Infamous Charges Made Against Him by James Gordon Bennett, William L. Stone and Others. New York: J. Winchester, New World Press, 1844.

————. *A Second Letter on the Moral Causes That Have Produced the Evil Spirit of the Times*: Addressed to the Honorable James Harper, Mayor of New York, Including a Vindication of the Author from the Infamous Charges Made Against Him by James Gordon Bennett, William L. Stone and Others. New York: J. Winchester, New World Press, 1844.

Humphrey, Edward Frank. *Nationalism and Religion in America 1774–1789*. Boston: Chipman Law, 1924.

Hunter, Earle L. *A Sociological Analysis of Certain Types of Patriotism*. New York: Columbia University Press, 1932.

Ireland, John. *The Church and Modern Society*. St. Paul, Minn.: Pioneer Press, 1905.

Jones, Tracey K., Jr. *Our Mission Today*: The Beginnings of a New Age. New York: World Outlook Press, 1963.

Kallen, Horace. *Culture and Democracy in the United States*. New York: Boni and Liveright, 1924.

Keller, James. *Three Minutes a Day*. New York: Macmillan, 1949.

————. *You Can Change the World!* New York: Longmans, Green, 1948.

Kelly, Thomas (ed.). *The Glories of the Catholic Church*. 3 vols. New York: John Duffy, 1894.

Kennedy, John J. *Catholicism, Nationalism and Democracy in Argentina*. Notre Dame, Ind.: University of Notre Dame Press, 1958.

Kinzer, Donald L. *An Episode in Anti-Catholicism*: The American Protective Association. Seattle: University of Washington Press, 1964.

Koch, Adrienne. *Power, Morals, and the Founding Fathers*. Ithaca, N.Y.: Cornell University Press, 1961.

Kohn, Hans. *The Age of Nationalism*: The First Era of Global History. New York: Harper, 1962.

————. *American Nationalism*: An Interpretative Essay. New York: Macmillan, 1957.

————. *Nationalism: Its Meaning and History*. Princeton, N.J.: Van Nostrand, Anvil Original, 1955.

Leclercq, Jacques. *The Christian and World Integration*. New York: Hawthorn Books, 1963.

Lewy, Guenter. *The Catholic Church and Nazi Germany*. New York: McGraw Hill, 1964.

*The Life of Archbishop Hughes*. Philadelphia: T. B. Peterson, 1864.

Lipset, Seymour M. *The First New Nation*: The United States in Historical and Comparative Perspective. New York: Basic Books, 1963.

Malinowski, Bronislaw. *Magic, Science and Religion*. Garden City, N.Y.: Doubleday Anchor, 1948.

Mannheim, Karl. *Ideology and Utopia*: An Introduction to the Sociology of Knowledge. Translated by Louis Wirth and Edward Shils. New York: Harcourt, Brace, Harvest Book, 1936.

Marty, Martin E. *The New Shape of American Religion*. New York: Harper, 1959.

———. *Varieties of Unbelief*. New York: Holt, Rinehart and Winston, 1964.

Marx, Karl, and Engels, Friedrich. *On Religion*. With an introduction by Reinhold Niebuhr. New York: Schocken Books, 1964.

McAvoy, Thomas T. (ed.). *Roman Catholicism and the American Way of Life*. Notre Dame, Ind.: University of Notre Dame Press, 1960.

McDonald, Donald. *Religion:* One of a Series of Interviews on the American Character. Santa Barbara: Fund for the Republic, 1962.

McKenna, Richard. *The Sand Pebbles*. New York: Crest Books, 1964.

McSorley, Joseph. *Father Hecker and His Friends*. St. Louis: Herder, 1952.

Mead, Sidney E. *The Lively Experiment*: The Shaping of Christianity in America. New York: Harper and Row, 1963.

Melville, Annabelle M. *John Carroll of Baltimore*. New York: Scribner, 1955.

Merton, Robert K. *Social Theory and Social Structure.* Glencoe, Ill.: The Free Press, 1949.

Mills, C. Wright. *The Sociological Imagination.* New York: Oxford University Press, 1959.

Moynihan, James H. *The Life of Archbishop Ireland.* New York: Harper, 1953.

Mulder, William, and Mortensen, A. Russell (ed.). *Among the Mormons.* New York: Knopf, 1958.

Murrow, Edward R. *This I Believe.* New York: Simon and Schuster, 1953.

*Nationalism*: A Report by a Study Group of Members of the Royal Institute of International Affairs. London: Oxford University Press, 1939.

*The National Pastorals of the American Hierarchy (1792–1919).* With a foreword, notes and index by Peter Guilday. Washington, D.C.: National Catholic Welfare Conference, 1923.

Niebuhr, Reinhold. *Christianity and Power Politics.* New York: Scribner, 1952.

———. *The Irony of American History.* New York: Scribner, 1952.

Niebuhr, Reinhold, and Heimert, Alan. *A Nation So Conceived.* New York: Scribner, 1963.

Nisbet, Robert A. *The Quest for Community.* New York: Oxford University Press, 1953.

Nottingham, Elizabeth K. *Religion and Society.* New York: Random House, 1954.

O'Connell, William. *Recollections of Seventy Years.* Boston: Houghton Mifflin, 1934.

O'Dea, Thomas F. *American Catholic Dilemma*: An Inquiry into the Intellectual Life. New York: Sheed and Ward, 1958.

O'Faolain, Sean. *King of the Beggars*: A Life of Daniel O'Connell. New York: Viking, 1938.

Otto, Rudolf. *The Idea of the Holy*: An Inquiry into the Non-Rational Factor in the Idea of the Divine and its Relation to the Rational. Translated by John W. Harvey. New York: Oxford University Press, Galaxy, 1958.

Parkes, Henry. *The American Experience*. New York: Knopf, 1947.

Parsons, Talcott. *Essays in Sociological Theory*. 2d ed. revised. New York: Free Press of Glencoe paperback, 1964.

————. *Structure of Social Action*. Glencoe, Ill.: The Free Press, 1949.

Perry, Ralph Barton. *Puritanism and Democracy*. New York: Vanguard, 1944.

Richards, Audrey I. *Hunger and Work in a Savage Tribe*. Chicago: The Free Press, 1948.

Ryan, Alvan S. *The Brownson Reader*. New York: Kenedy, 1955.

Salisbury, W. Seward. *Religion in American Culture*. Homewood, Ill.: Dorsey, 1964.

Schneider, Louis. *Religion, Culture and Society*. New York: Wiley, 1964.

Schneider, Louis, and Dornbusch, Sanford. *Popular Religion*: Inspirational Books in America. Chicago: University of Chicago Press, 1958.

Selltiz, Claire, *et al*. *Research Methods in Social Relations*. 2d ed. revised. New York: Holt, Rinehart and Winston, 1959.

Shafer, Boyd C. *Nationalism: Interpreters and Interpretations*. 2d ed. Washington, D.C.: Service Center for Teachers of History, 1963.

————. *Nationalism: Myth and Reality*. New York: Harcourt, Brace, 1955.

Shannon, William. *The American Irish*. New York: Macmillan, 1963.

Shea, John Gilmary. *The Cross and the Flag*: Our Church and Country. New York: Catholic Historical League of America, 1899.

————. *The Hierarchy of the Catholic Church in the United States*. New York: Office of Catholic Publications, 1886.

Shea, John Gilmary. *Life and Times of the Most Rev. John Carroll.* Vol. II of *The History of the Catholic Church in the United States.* New York: Shea, 1888.

Sheen, Fulton J. *Peace of Soul.* New York: Whittlesey House, 1949.

Silvert, K. H. (ed.). *Expectant Peoples*: Nationalism and Development. New York: Random House, 1963.

Smith, Bradford. *Why We Behave Like Americans.* Philadelphia: Lippincott, 1957.

Smith, H. Shelton, Handy, Robert T., and Loetscher, Lefferts A. *American Christianity*: An Historical Interpretation with Representative Documents. Vol. I: 1607–1820. Vol. II: 1820–1960. New York: Scribner, 1963.

Smith, James Ward, and Jamison, A. Leland. *The Shaping of American Religion.* Vol. I: *Religion in American Life.* Princeton, N.J.: Princeton University Press, 1961.

Smith, John Talbot. *History of the Catholic Church in New York.* 2 vols. New York and Boston: Hall and Locke Company, 1905.

Spalding, John Lancaster. *Essays and Reviews.* New York: Catholic Publication Society, 1877.

———. *Glimpses of Truth.* Chicago: McClurg, 1903.

———. *Lectures and Discourses.* New York: Catholic Publication Society, 1882.

———. *Opportunity and Other Essays and Addresses.* Chicago: McClurg, 1901.

———. *The Religious Mission of the Irish People.* 6th ed. New York: Christian Press Association, 1897.

———. *Socialism and Labor.* Chicago: McClurg, 1902.

———. *Thoughts and Theories of Life and Education.* Chicago: McClurg, 1910.

Spellman, Francis J. *Action This Day.* New York: Scribner, 1943.

———. *The Foundling.* New York: Scribner, 1951.

———. *No Greater Love.* New York: Scribner, 1945.

———. *Prayers and Poems.* Scribner, 1946.

————. *The Risen Soldier*. New York: Macmillan, 1944.

————. *The Road to Victory*. New York: Scribner, 1942.

————. *What America Means to Me*. New York: Scribner, 1953.

Sweeney, David Francis. *Life of John Lancaster Spalding*. New York: Herder and Herder, 1966.

Thomas, John L., S.J. *Religion and the American People*. Westminster, Md.: Newman, 1963.

Timasheff, Nicholas S. *Sociological Theory*: Its Nature and Its Growth. 2d ed. revised. New York: Random House, 1957.

Timasheff, Nicholas S., and Facey, Paul W. *Sociology*: A Sociological Analysis. Milwaukee: Bruce, 1949.

Tocqueville, Alexis de. *Democracy in America*. 2 vols. New York: Knopf, 1945.

Troeltsch, Ernst. *The Social Teaching of the Christian Churches*. 2 vols. Translated by Olive Wyon. New York: Harper Torchbooks, 1960.

U.S. Congress. *Inaugural Addresses of the Presidents of the United States*. House Document no. 540. 82nd Cong., 2d Sess., 1952.

Van der Leeuw, G. *Religion in Essence and Manifestation*: A Study of Phenomenology. 2 vols. Translated by J. E. Turner with Appendices incorporating the additions to the second German edition by Hans H. Penner. New York: Harper Torchbooks, 1963.

Von der Mehden, Fred R. *Religion and Nationalism in Southeast Asia*. Madison, Wis.: University of Wisconsin Press, 1963.

Wach, Joachim. *Sociology of Religion*. Chicago: University of Chicago, Phoenix Books, 1944.

Warner, W. Lloyd. *The Family of God*. New Haven: Yale University Paperback, 1961.

Wayman, Dorothy G. *Cardinal O'Connell of Boston*. New York: Farrar, Straus and Young, 1955.

Weber, Max. *The Sociology of Religion*. Translated by Ephraim Fischoff. Boston: Beacon Paperback, 1964.

Will, Allen Sinclair. *Life of Cardinal Gibbons*. New York: Dutton. 1922.

Williams, Robin. *American Society*: A Sociological Interpretation. 2d ed. revised. New York: Knopf, 1960.

Wittke, Carl Frederick. *The Irish in America*. Baton Rouge: Louisiana State University Press, 1956.

Wright, John J. *National Patriotism in Papal Teaching*. Westminster, Md.: Newman, 1943.

Yinger, J. Milton. *Sociology Looks at Religion*. New York: Macmillan, 1963.

Zahn, Gordon Charles. *A Descriptive Study of the Social Backgrounds of Conscientious Objectors in Civilian Public Service during World War II*. Washington, D.C.: Catholic University of America Press, 1953.

————. *German Catholics and Hitler's Wars*. New York: Sheed and Ward, 1961.

————. *In Solitary Witness*: The Life and Death of Franz Jagerstatter. New York: Holt, Rinehart, and Winston, 1964.

Zwierlein, Frederick J. *The Life and Letters of Bishop McQuaid*. 3 vols. Rochester, N.Y.: Art Print Shop, 1927.

## ARTICLES AND PERIODICALS

Barry, Colman J., O.S.B. "Some Roots of American Nativism," *The Catholic Historical Review*, XLIV (July 1958), 137–146.

Bell, Daniel. "Beyond the Melting Pot," *Commentary*, XXXVII (January 1964), 74–76.

Bellah, Robert N. "Religious Evolution," *American Sociological Review*, XXIX (June 1964), 358–374.

Bernd, Daniel. "Did Goldwater Lose?" *The New Republic*, CLI (December 5, 1964), 8–10.

Callahan, Daniel. "The New Pluralism: From Nostalgia to Reality," *Commonweal*, LXXIX (September 6, 1963), 527–530.

Catton, Bruce. "The Unfinished Business of the Civil War," *New York Times Magazine*, April 4, 1965, 28–29.

Furfey, Paul H. "Curse of Nationalism," *Catholic World*, CLVI (March 1943), 652–657.

Gleason, Philip. "Pluralism and the New Pluralism," *America*, CX (March 7, 1964), 308–312.

Hertz, Frederick. "The Nature of Nationalism," *Social Forces*, XIX (March 1941), 409–415.

Higham, John. "Another Look at Nativism," *The Catholic Historical Review*, XLIV (July 1958), 147–158.

Ichheiser, Gustav. "Some Psychological Obstacles to an Understanding between the Nations," *Journal of Abnormal Psychology*, XXXVI (July 1941), 428–432.

Kenny, Lawrence J., S.J. "America—A Land of Destiny," *The Catholic Mind*, XXV (September 8, 1927), 321–340. Quoted material reprinted with permission of *The Catholic Mind*, The Monthly Review of Christian Thought and Documentation, 106 W. 56th Street, New York, N.Y.

LaFarge, John. "Three Main Causes of Nationalism," *Thought*, IX (September 1934), 181–192.

Lazerwitz, Bernard, and Rowitz, Louis. "The Three-Generations Hypothesis," *American Journal of Sociology*, LXIX (March 1964), 529–538.

Meehan, Thomas F. "Catholic Activities in Our Two Great Wars," *Catholic World*, CVII (July 1918), 444–463.

Mitchell, M. Marion. "Emile Durkheim and the Philosophy of Nationalism," *Political Science Quarterly*, XLVI (March 1931), 87–106.

O'Brien, William V. "Morality, Nuclear War, and the Schema on the Church in the Modern World," *CAIP News*, October 1964.

O'Dea, Thomas F. "American Catholics and International Life," *Social Order*, X (June 1960), 243–265.

Terrill, Ross. "A Trip to China," *The New Republic*, CLII (January 2, 1965), 9–11.

Traynor, George. "Charter for Laymen, 1822," *Commonweal*, LXXXI (December 18, 1964), 418–420.

Vawter, Bruce, C. M. "The Beast from the Sea," *Commonweal*, LXXX (May 22, 1964), 253–256.


## OTHER SOURCES

Archives of the Archdiocese of New York.
Cahoon, Sister M. Janelle. *Tensions and Dilemmas Facing Organized Christianity in the Contemporary United States as Recognized in Official Church Statements.* Unpublished Ph.D. dissertation, Fordham University, 1963.

# Index